GIRLS' GUIDE TO FOOTY

GIRLS' GUIDE TO FOOTY
A BANTAM BOOK
First published in Australia and New Zealand in 1996 by Bantam

Copyright © Tracey Holmes, 1996

National Library of Australia
Cataloguing-in -Publication Entry

Holmes, Tracey
Girls' Guide to Footy

ISBN 1 86359 779 4

1. Football – Handbooks, manuals etc. 2. Rugby Union football – Handbooks, manuals etc. 3. Rugby League football – Handbooks, manuals etc. 4. Soccer – Handbooks, manuals etc. 5. Australian football – Handbooks, manuals etc. I. Title

796.33

Bantam books are published by:
Transworld Publishers (Aust) Pty Limited
15-25 Helles Ave, Moorebank, NSW 2170
Transworld Publishers (NZ) Limited
3 William Pickering Drive, Albany, Auckland
Transworld Publishers (UK) Limited
61-63 Uxbridge Road, Ealing, London, W5 5SA
Bantam Doubleday Dell Publishing Group Inc
1540 Broadway, New York, New York 10036

Design by Reno Design Group / Graham Rendoth 15100
Design production; Wayne Boyd, Craig Pinney, Ingrid Urh
Photography by Greg Barrett
Illustrations by Fiona Tromans / Every Picture Tells a Story
Diagrams by Craig Pinney
Printed by Australian Print Group, Victoria
10 9 8 7 6 5 4 3 2 1

GIRLS' GUIDE TO FOOTY

Tracey Holmes

BANTAM BOOKS
SYDNEY • AUCKLAND • TORONTO • NEW YORK • LONDON

THANK YOU

Thanks to Peter Wilkins who knew this book off by heart before it was even published.

Thanks to Rory McDonald for his contacts, stories and interviews.

Thanks to all the players, coaches, officials and their wives who contributed.

Thanks to Laura Paterson for making me think I could do this.

Thanks to Transworld for giving me the opportunity to write this book.

Thank you for reading this book.

CONTENTS

1 GET

INTO IT!

INTRODUCTION

O pen your mind. No forethought, no barriers, no biases. Now paint a lush green field, with blue sky running in an arc from one side of the ground to the other. The sun burns hot and the earth feels spongy between your feet. Breathe in the fresh air of an autumn day.

Now throw in a handful of Greek gods. Finely sculptured athletes carved by someone with the artistic talents of Michelangelo.

Welcome to the world of footy...whichever code you choose!

Well, OK, it's not always bright sunshine – it's often bucketing down, and there may be a wind chill factor of minus fifty. It's not always a green pasture; it's sometimes more like a mudbath. And yes, I agree, some of the players are more like prehistoric men than masterpieces but, hey, that's what makes the game so real.

Some of you will already be addicted to football. For you, this book can be used as a quick reference guide. Others may be dipping their toes into new waters – congratulations, you're about to enter a whole new world, one which can be as much fun as any other you've previously enjoyed.

Regrettably, there will be those of you who are flipping through this book without the slightest interest. You will be pouting. You may even be annoyed that somebody had the audacity to think you would get anything from it. If you fit into this category, re-read paragraph one.

It's easy to feel turned off by something that seems incredibly involved and complicated – with enough statistics to bamboozle the world's greatest mathematical minds. But wait! It's really not all that frightening. A general understanding of what the game is about, some hints on how to feel a part of the scene and you'll be out there on the hill at your local ground cheering on the team along with all the other fanatics.

There are certainly plenty of experts out there in the big, bad world of footy who will spend their days trying to impress you with their thorough knowledge of the game at every level...from schoolboy teams through to the professional ranks of international stardom. They recite neverending reams of stats, figures, scores and players' names from centuries past and then ask you what you thought of the first-ever drawn Test between Papua New Guinea and the Zambesi Reserves.

Don't feel out of your depth. Just tell these people that you'd rather count passing cars than continue talking with them. That usually shuts them up for a while and lets you get on with enjoying the footy.

'I find that the majority of complaints I hear about football are from people who don't actually know what's going on.'
Johanna Sweet, **Sports Presenter**

Most of these 'experts' should be put through football's academy of public relations because they are the ultimate turn-off. Ignore them and know that you can enjoy the game at any level you choose, whether it's as a one-off excursion or whether you plan to become a walking CD-ROM of the sport.

Football is like dessert. You have to partake of it at least every so often and the chances are the more you have, the more you want. The delights are plentiful. The mere fact that you are outdoors in all kinds of conditions gives you a sense of adventure. The energy surrounding sport is a turn-on.

OLYMPIC GOLD!

Australia's only gold medal at the 1908 Olympic Games held in London, was won by the Wallabies Rugby Union team who became Olympians for a day during their tour of the British Isles. The only other team entered in the Olympic rugby competition was England. Australia won 32–3.

Some grounds have an almost visible aura: the Maracana Stadium in Brazil, for example, is the world's biggest footy field, (used mostly for soccer) and takes a crowd of up to 205,000. A moat surrounds the playing area and referees and linesmen get onto the field via manholes with tunnels offering an escape from the often frightening crowd. Ninety minutes of football in Rio is one of the most exhilarating experiences on earth. Jot down the idea for a future holiday – it would be well worth it.

As well as the atmosphere at any football game there are the physical surroundings. There are colours and voices, screaming fans, excited kids, and vibrations crawling up from your seat or the ground you are standing on so that every tackle made is a thump that you can feel.

An appreciation of the physicality of the game is easy when you're at the ground – it's a sensation radio or television can never portray. You can take your place on the hill, where the most vocal of supporters gather to relieve their anxieties after a week at work, or you can choose a grandstand seat offering a more comfortable view of the action but without so many of the surrounding sensations. If you 'know' somebody you might luck into a gold (member) ticket, complete with champagne service.

The band is playing, there are girls dancing, parachutists appear, there is a buzz that makes you almost nervous on the inside. Then the players run from the tunnel and that buzz bursts deep inside you like a spark turning to a flame.

Look at the players. They are so carefully designed. Their legs dynamically carved – the wingers and centres for sprinting, the forwards for power in attack and defence. Shoulders as broad and straight as the horizon and hands that could close around you like a flower's bud.

The authority of the whistle is ignited by the referee's breath and the game is underway. There are speedsters, there are the power players, there are the tricksters and the tacticians. Some play well, others look good. And there are those who have it all.

Tony Lockett in aussie rules, Laurie Daley in rugby league, George Gregan in rugby union and Ned Zelic in soccer. These are men that gamble with a game. They have honed their skills to perfection and then added a spice called creativity. They bamboozle the opposition, frighten their coaches and thrill the crowd. They are the heroes. They are the big money earners and they are responsible for pushing the limits of the game to ever increasing heights of talent, strength and glory.

It is these star players who inspire the urge for 'super' leagues. It is men of this calibre who can persuade multinational corporations to invest millions in one code. It is their skill that provides the entertainment that the public will pay good money for. They are the champions that motivate our kids to play the game and maybe even tempt them to look at football as a career.

Alongside the players, there are the coaching staff, sitting huddled in a group, either smirking knowingly at their team's gladiatorial dominance or with their heads in their hands looking as if doomsday had just arrived.

You can gauge a lot about a coach by his or her performance during the game. The strong silent types like aussie rules' Kevin Sheedy keep you intrigued. For the rompy-stompy tough guy approach watch soccer's Frank Arok who'll fill you with aggression. Then there's Tomato Tom, Tommy Raudonikis from rugby league, who really is the battler's battler. Watching Tommy during a game is like watching an Australian soldier in the trenches of war. He has that 'fight to the death' approach written all over him and by gee, it spurs a team of ordinary players on to some mighty things.

At some stage you will notice a whole heap of other blokes running on and off the ground whenever they feel the need. They are normally dressed in tight-fitting t-shirts, baggy Country Road style cotton shorts and baseball caps. These guys are the trainers, and they run around like rabbits on an open field, darting here, darting there. Their apparent purpose is to shuffle drink bottles on and off the ground so players don't dehydrate.

In fact they are the James Bonds of the team, the 007 secret agents charged with the mission of relaying coaches' messages to the players while the game is still in progress. Messages often run along the lines of 'that tip you gave me in race six at Flemington has just won, but I forgot to put your money on it'.

This normally lifts a player's work rate by at least 120% and therefore achieves the effect the coach was after. If you watch carefully, you can also sometimes lip-read the messages being mouthed by the trainers. It's more fun, though, to lip-read the players' messages back to the coach.

Then, of course, there's the umpire or referee and his team of workers. The refs are probably the fittest people on the field because they are continuously running with the leading players. Rugby league refs have been clocked running almost 42 kilometres in one game (the equivalent of an Olympic marathon) but unlike other marathon runners, they still have to have their wits about them. They are making decisions, scrutinising players and dictating the pace of the game.

It's easy to fall in love with football. Let it happen. Pick a player or a team that appeals to you. Pick a fast runner, a strong tackler, a good-looking backside. Pick a coloured jersey that you like, or a

THE CONVERSION OF TRACEY HOLMES

I was converted to footy after the age of eight when my dad took me to watch a game of rugby league between Manly and Parramatta – traditional rivals of the greatest kind.

Manly Sea Eagles represented everything about the Northern Beaches of Sydney – surfboards, beach parties and good times. The Parramatta Eels represented everything about the Western Suburbs – thongs, panel vans and tattoos. My cousins were wild Parra supporters, and arguments over which of 'our' teams was better dominated any family get-together.

Something changed the afternoon my dad took me to Brooky (Brookvale) oval, home of the Manly Sea Eagles, because it was there that I became a woman.

Watching the two sides run out onto the ground I saw the perfect man. I understood, for the first time, what the majesty of an athlete was all about. Ray Price – flowing blond hair, a bald patch, missing front teeth and shoulders to die for, but he played for Parramatta.

My heart wrenched throughout the game as I yelled all the phrases a Manly supporter should yell, but inside all I wanted to shout was 'Pricey – you're a legend'.

So before my first decade in life was complete, I knew what football was all about. I knew what it was to be in love, and I knew that I would never again bag my cousins for being 'westies' because the greatest rugby league player of all time came from their turf.

team name that inspires you. Follow the team your friends follow and make it your mission to learn something about the side each week. Single out one thing that you can relate to and build your knowledge of the game around that. Soon your taste buds will be tantalised and you'll be hungry to learn about other aspects of the game, maybe even about the other codes!

A BRIEF HISTORY

There is argument over which game of football actually came first according to Darwin's theory of evolution.

It's been said that when man first discovered a stone, he kicked it. So perhaps it was soccer that really got the ball rolling. (Sorry, no more bad jokes!)

Balls have been found in ancient Egyptian tombs. The Normans used to decapitate their foes and kick their heads through the streets as a form of celebration. The Romans developed a game of football to build the athleticism of their soldiers, and in 1314 King Edward II tried to ban football because it was taking over modern day life!

People would play it from sunrise to sunset, limbs would be broken, houses smashed and, in rare instances, deaths occurred. On the other hand, though, a kind of football called Marn-Grook was played by the Aborigines to restore peace between tribes.

Soccer is officially regarded as the first pure form of football played throughout Europe and the British Isles. Then in 1823, at a school in the English town of Rugby, a student named William Webb Ellis got sick and tired of kicking the ball so he picked it up and ran with it. Rugby union was born.

We still play for the Webb Ellis Trophy, now known as the World Cup, which South Africa won in emotional scenes in 1995. It wasn't until 1895 that a breakaway group formed the 'rugby league' for players who needed to be compensated for time lost at work while they were playing the game for their clubs.

Meanwhile, Australian Rules football had been born in 1858. Victorian miners had come up with their own blend of footy – a mixture of rugby and Gaelic football to keep the cricketers both entertained and physically fit during the off season.

It's by no means a static environment, either. Rules continue to change in each game, and there is even some talk of a hybrid game being developed because of the on-going media war aimed at controlling the various sports. The cost of buying rights to each code of football is astronomical. Millions of dollars for individual tournaments puts football out of reach for most local radio and television stations and coverage is being left to the multi-national conglomerates who can televise games internationally.

Media magnate Rupert Murdoch is paying prices that few others could afford. It has been suggested that once he owns the rights to all of them, on a global scale, we will see the merging of all codes into one new game – Murdoch Ball. Now that's the measure of someone who's made it!

it's easiest if you only watch the top teams until you get the hang of it. Any sport at its best is engaging.

Kate Paton, Sports Reporter

Little offshoots of the sport also appear every now and then. Touch footy has overtaken netball as Australia's highest participation sport. American football, or gridiron, also developed from the original game of soccer. Internationally, women's football leagues are becoming stronger and throughout America, Europe and China women's soccer is starting to challenge the men's game in terms of participation, financial support and crowd attraction. As men's leagues continue to get further and further out of range for potential sponsors, the women's games are offering an attractive alternative.

The Australian Women's Soccer team toured China and South America as a warm-up to the 1995 World Cup and were shocked when upwards of 40,000 spectators arrived for individual games. Men's internationals in Australia struggle to draw crowds as large as that!

Football these days appeals to all groups. The old class system no longer exists. All four codes are enjoyed in Australia and all can lay claim to being international, though to varying degrees. There is no longer a specific attitude associated with each code other than the continual search for professionalism and excellence to which everybody, regardless of background, education and lifestyle, can relate.

So, it's time to lace up those boots, whack in the mouthguard, and prepare for the game. On your marks, get set, let's play football!

BASICS

In the 1990s we know how to live life. We know how to cope with environment-friendly kitchens and eco-friendly rubbish bins. We are aware that every household in our street represents a different minority group and we are happy in the knowledge that we tolerate all-comers. But, at the risk of sounding politically incorrect, we have one huge admission to make: no matter what we say, or how we say it, we just can't seem to get on with the SNAF brigade.

These Sensitive New Age Footyheads seem like regular people until you get involved with them on a day-to-day basis. Then you discover that there is only one 'high' in their week – the footy. They then spend the next six days building up to their next peak.

There are no old wives' tales on how to cope with a SNAF because, believe it or not, all the old wives gave up trying to cope. They either converted to Footyheadism or bailed out. Bailing out is the easy option, but conversion is the preferred alternative and, with a little persistence, you'll find that it really is worth the effort.

THE EASY CONVERSION TECHNIQUE

1. Don't be turned off by know-alls

It's impossible to know everything about any one code. If you meet somebody that claims to know it all, you've met a liar.

2. Forget the rule book

Nobody learns how to play a game by studying a rule book. The great rugby winger David Campese has never read the laws of his own game, so why should we?

3. To become respected football critics we need to experience the sensations of football for ourselves

You need to know how it feels in the pit of your stomach before a grand final, how it feels to have your face rubbed in the dirt by a 300 kg opponent, and you need to have tears of celebration running down your cheeks and into your toothless mouth after winning the World Cup.

By following these three easy steps you will soon understand what Footyheadism is all about...and isn't it great to know that in the 1990s, in this era of virtual reality, you can experience it all by reading one little book!

You must realise, that having committed yourself to becoming a Footyhead, you are entering 'sacred turf' [see glossary]. To progress beyond this stage and fully qualify as a member of the Footyhead Brigade you must publicly declare your intentions within seven days of reading this chapter. You have three choices:

1. Start up a footy conversation with someone at work/ the pub/school/uni.

2. Phone the coach of your local club and offer your thoughts on how the team can improve before next weekend's 'big game' [see glossary].

3. Call your local radio station next time they have football talkback and ask them if they're disappointed in the way the game is being played these days.
(True footyheads can talk about this topic for days!)

Unlike other groups or clubs or religions, Footyheadism offers you endless choices. For starters, pick the code you'd most like to learn about. Here are some guidelines that might help...

SOCCER

For those with no arms – all the skill is with your feet and your head unless you are Mark Bosnich! Mark is one of the many Australians on million dollar contracts overseas, and he is also Australia's number one choice for goalkeeper whenever internationals are played. His availability, though, depends very much on whether his club will release him to play for his country.

Mark is magic – what he can do to stop a ball will mesmerise you. He dives and twists and contorts into all sorts of shapes just to stop some other bloke scoring. Goalkeepers are the only players that can display such techniques because they are the

---

THE BASICS

■ Played in two halves of 45 minutes each with a halftime break of five minutes.

■ 11 players per team allowed on the field at one time.

■ One player in goal to stop opposition scoring.

■ The rest of the team combine in a pre-determined formation to attack, defend and strike at goal.

■ THE AIM is to score more goals than the opposition by kicking goals or penalties, each worth one point.

■ If scores are level at fulltime there are three possible ways to obtain a result:
EXTRA TIME – two halves of 15 minutes.
SUDDEN DEATH – the first team to score after fulltime wins.

PENALTY SHOOT-OUT – each team can kick for goal five times, and the team with most goals wins.
If the scores are still locked, teams take alternative penalty kicks. The first team to score wins.
The option taken depends on the organisers – it is determined before the start of the competition.
In early round matches, a draw is usually sufficient. It's only when a winner MUST be found that one of the above three options will be used.

■ SKILLS of the game revolve around kicking – moving the ball forward, sideways and backwards in attack, and, in defence, being able to tackle or steal the ball from the opponents.

only ones allowed to use their arms and hands. Overacting is also viewed favourably – in fact the international body controlling soccer, Federation Internationale de Football Association (or FIFA), even has a 'celebration of goal' rule.

If you are attracted to big-money sports, rather than following the local amateur tiddlywinks club, you can't go past soccer – contracts start at about $1.2 million and go up to $40 million for World Cup stars. Players won't see much of it though, because at this level they'll have a couple of agents, two or three managers, personal medical staff and their own airline, all of which will account for 98% of their wage. Then there's tax – so they'll actually be running at a loss! But, hey, if you make it on the news every night, are pictured in women's magazines every week and get sent fan mail from around the world, it's probably worth being broke.

RECOGNISABLE FEATURES

■ *A round ball: not the elongated ball used in the other codes of football.*

■ *A netted goal area: the area between the upright posts and the cross bar is sealed with a net. If the whole of the ball crosses the goal line and lands anywhere inside the netted area, it's deemed a goal.*

■ *One player will be wearing a different uniform from the rest of his team mates. He is the 'goalie' and he wears padded gloves and a colourful long-sleeved jersey to give him protection as he dives to stop the opposition's ball going into the goal area.*

■ *Hands are not used by any player except the goalie.*

■ *ACADEMY AWARD-WINNING ACTING: because the opportunities to score are low, teams try their best to win penalties or free kicks. If an opponent accidentally kicks a player in the shins the player usually collapses in agony, acts as though he's suffered a major coronary and hopes the referee awards a penalty or free kick, so his team can kick for goal. NOTE: A penalty is given for a deliberate foul inside the penalty area.*

A free kick, on the other hand, is given for an infringement outside the penalty area.

■ *FREE KICKS: There are two types – direct and indirect. A direct free kick can be booted straight home for a goal, whereas a goal can't be scored from an indirect free kick unless it is played or touched by a team mate.*

RUGBY UNION

If you like bonding, rugby's the code for you. You will witness incredible sporting feats known as 'rucks' and 'mauls' in which a group of team mates and some of the opposition run together and cuddle while the ball hides in the middle of the huddle and nobody is really sure who's got it.

This code was the 'true' amateur code – only the very rich could afford to play it until they realised they could become even richer if they turned professional.

THE BASICS

■ *Two halves of 40 minutes, with a ten minute break.*

■ *Fifteen players per team allowed on the field at a time*
  – eight forwards and seven backs.

■ *FORWARDS aim to win the ball.*

■ *BACKS must try to beat the opposition and score.*

■ *THE AIM is to score more points than the opposition.*

Points are awarded in four ways:

TRY – 5 points

KICKED CONVERSION OF THE TRY – 2 points

PENALTY GOAL – 3 points

DROP GOAL/FIELD GOAL – 3 points.

■ *SKILLS include accuracy of kicking, precision with*
  passing, power in tackling.

RECOGNISABLE FEATURES

■ *LINEOUTS: when the forwards from both teams line up alongside each other, perpendicular to the touchline (or sideline) and try to grab the ball as it's thrown into the gap between the two teams.*

■ *RUCKS: when a player is tackled to the ground he must release the ball. The teams then form what looks like a scrum over the top of the ball and try to gain possession by hooking it back into their line of play.*

■ *MAULS: the upright version of rucks. If a player is tackled but not brought to the ground, his team mates form around him, the opposition form opposite and a wrestle for the ball ensues.*

RUGBY LEAGUE

Along with rugby, the only game in the world where the ball is thrown backwards with the aim of going forwards.

Emotional people are attracted to rugby league because of all the physical contact in the game. Players are always more than willing to lend the opposition a shoulder to cry on...they are so thoughtful they normally offer their shoulder first. The pain of it all leaves the opposition in tears.

THE BASICS

- *Two halves of 40 minutes, with a break of ten minutes.*
- *Thirteen players per team on the field at a time – 6 forwards, 7 backs.*
- *FORWARDS are the big men used for making ground in attack and they are the first line of defence.*
- *BACKS are speedy runners used to score.*
- *THE AIM is to score more points than the opposition.*
- *Points are awarded in four ways: TRY – 4 points KICKED CONVERSION OF THE TRY – 2 points PENALTY GOAL – 2 points DROP GOAL/FIELD GOAL – 1 point*
- *SKILLS are accurate kicking, precision passing, powerful tackling and deceptive running. Like rugby, many tactical plays are used to break up the opposition's defences.*

RECOGNISABLE FEATURES

- *DUMMY HALVES: unlike rugby union, there are no rucks and mauls. Once a player has been tackled by one or more of his opponents, he stands up and, with one foot, rolls the ball behind him to a team mate. This team mate is in a temporary position called a 'dummy half'.*
- *THE SIX TACKLE RULE: each team is only allowed six tackles with which to score a try. On the penultimate tackle, the referee will raise his left arm, indicating that five tackles have been made. The kicker of the attacking team then usually boots the ball as deeply as possible into the opposition's territory, giving them further to run once they gain possession of the ball.*

AUSSIE RULES

If you like chaos, aussie rules is your game. It is also known as aerial ping-pong because of the players' ability to apparently walk on air in order to catch high balls before kicking them home for a goal. At any one time there are 43 people running around the ground – and nobody knows what anyone else is up to!

There are 18 players on each team and seven umpires who are supposed to adjudicate. Also, if you are a fan of hotpants, look no further. Aussie rules fashion dictates that players wear the skimpiest, tightest, leave-nothing-to-the-imagination shorts so that the opposition, and the crowd, is permanently distracted, and even a basic primary school education has taught us that taking your eye off the ball is dangerous!

THE BASICS

- **Four quarters of 20 minutes, with a break of five minutes after the first and third quarters and a break of 20 minutes at halftime.**
- **Eighteen players per team allowed on the ground at one time – 6 backs, 6 centreline and on-ball players and 6 forwards.**
- **BACKS play close to their opponents to stop them scoring.**
- **FORWARDS try to shake off their markers in order to kick goals.**
- **THE AIM is to score more points than the opposition by kicking goals.**
- **GOALS are kicked between the two centre posts and are worth six points, unless the ball is touched by an opposition player or hits the post. It's then only worth one point. However, a second chance is given for scoring: if the ball fails to go through the goalposts it could roll through the smaller posts on either side. This is called a BEHIND and counts as one point. So an aussie rules score looks like this:**
  FOOTYHEADS – 12.20.92
  FOOTYBAGGERS – 0.1.1
  That is, the Footyheads kicked 12 goals (12 x 6 points = 72) and 20 behinds (20 points) to give them a total of 92 points, while the Footybaggers got only one behind for one point.
- **SKILLS involve accurate and powerful kicking, speed and the agility to jump and secure high balls, known as taking a mark.**

RECOGNISABLE FEATURES

- **Skin-tight shorts as opposed to the baggies preferred by other codes.**
- **Sleeveless jerseys which highlight the players' biceps and triceps.**
  (Long sleeves are worn on wet days and by skinny players.)
- **No cross bars on the goalposts. Goalposts sit between shorter posts, known as BEHIND POSTS.**
- **GOAL UMPIRES: these folk wear little white hats and long white coats. They use two white flags to signal the kicking of a goal. One flag is waved for a behind.**
- **THE PRESENCE OF UMPIRES Seven umpires control a game of AFL: – Three field umpires – Two on the boundary – Two goal umpires.**
- **Frenetic action: there are 43 people running around an AFL park – 18 players on either side plus the seven umpires. If you can keep up with all the action, you're a genius!**

Believe it or not, armed only with this knowledge, you are now prepared for battle. You can go along to any game of football, of whichever code you prefer, and be a sideline expert. You can sit amongst long-time supporters and act as if you've been following the game for years. Add these little extras to your armoury for even more protection:

1. **Fashionable footy clothing**
2. **The right lingo**
3. **A bit of research on one or two of the players**

FOOTY FASHIONS

Imagine turning up at a black tie function wearing a beach dress. Likewise, you wouldn't be too impressed arriving at a backyard barbie wearing your hot pink cocktail number. As with any other social occasion, dress is all important.

There are a several points to consider:

1. Who are you going with?

If it's with Cheryl and Bob from across the road, you can wear tracksuit pants just slightly better than theirs.

If it's with Melanie, one of the players' wives, then expect plenty of makeup and jewellery. Remember, this is work for her, and the degree of silver and gold being splashed around is evidence of how much her husband's contract is worth.

If you're going along with the boys from the pub, then pubwear is fine, but take a thick overcoat because those afternoon shadows and evening breezes can really go through you.

2. Where will you be seated?

'The Hill' requires ultra-casual gear (along the lines of a footy guernsey) that won't be affected by spilt beer or meat pie. Not that these items will be directed specifically at you, but in the heat of the moment when the crowd on the hill abuses the ref, you will no doubt be hit by flying objects. Don't let this type of behaviour upset you either – it's tradition. The hill is football's circus and there are plenty of clowns. They add colour, spark and personality to what can sometimes be a lacklustre game. Be prepared for a high decibel assault on the eardrums, too – we'll touch on some of the lines you must rehearse a little later on.

The grandstands require an upgrading in clothing. Perhaps good jeans, with a nice shirt and sporty coat. Leather boots are a must. If you'd like to show a passing interest in what's taking place in front of you, a casually draped scarf in the colours of the team you are supporting won't look out of place.

Private box seating is difficult. You have to look as if you are professional and deserve the chicken platter, but at the same time not looked overdressed. Remember, you are only at the football after all! The best disguise to hide any fashion fault is a well-tailored trench coat in navy blue. If you wear one of these, you are obviously a fashion guru, football guru and have money to boot. Enjoy the chicken.

Only on very special occasions will you be offered a seat directly behind the goal-posts. If you are given such an honour, you will need to prepare for days. Learn to knit, quickly. Know which team you will be supporting – you must wear a scarf, beanie, gloves and socks all in the team colours. You must paint up your face to look like Marcele Marceau, and find a drum that you can bash every time your team scores. Remember, sitting behind the goal area is the greatest of football privileges.

3. Where will you be going afterwards?

It's damn annoying to have your behind-the-goal-post outfit on when you bump into the local celebrity who invites you back to have dinner with the team sponsors and officials. The only way to overcome this kind of hiccup is to have an overnight bag of alternative outfits permanently stashed in your car. Being female, you probably already have this under control.

The most common post-match outing is a trip to the local footy club. Most of these have dress standards which you should check out before the match – some insist on dresses or slacks; others don't mind the chequered-shirt-and-ug-boot look.

On rare occasions, you will need some wet weather gear. Fold-up poncho raincoats are popular – you can just rip these out of the pocket in your tracksuit. Green garbage bags with a hole cut in the neck region are favoured on most hills. For those of you with gold member passes, the biggest umbrella you can find is a must. You won't need it, of course, because you will be under cover, but you'll turn heads if you arrive with a David Jones silver-plated brolly tucked nicely under the arm of your navy trench coat.

4. Code-specific dress regulations

SOCCER: Silk tracksuits are the go.
RUGBY UNION: Tweed jackets and conservative navy garments are most popular.

RUGBY LEAGUE: Big gold earrings, perms and bold lipstick are hits. Plus the team guernsey which is remarkably versatile. You can wear it with jeans, shorts, skirts or even over your favourite footy dress.

AUSSIE RULES: Anything goes at the truly Australian footy code. It must be remembered, though, that more than any other code, it's aussie rules that is a way of life (particularly if you live in Victoria). Going to the footy is not something you decide to do; it is mandatory. It takes careful consideration and must be done properly, so before you head out to the Carlton v Fitzroy clash, think carefully about your ensemble – others will be scrutinising your efforts.

There are a couple of clubs which have unwritten laws regarding their dress code. For example, Geelong supporters opt for the rural look – RM WIlliams moleskins; Melbourne is the old school tie brigade and cravats are popular, while Footscray goers favour flannelette shirts and moccasins.

THE RIGHT LINGO

Every generation carries with it new 'in' words or phrases. Football is exactly the same. Sometimes it's not just the jargon of the code, but of individual clubs. Certain incidents on the field may earn a player a new nickname. If you call him anything but that nickname, you might as well forget football altogether. But don't get disheartened – learning footy lingo is enjoyable! A little bit of abstract thinking, a colourful imagination and you might come up with the next buzzword at your local footy club!

On your first two or three outings just sit quietly in the crowd. You'll quickly pick up what to say and when to say it. The worst mistake you can make is to get a name slightly wrong. Footyheads are unforgiving in this department.

Lingo between codes differs, also. For example, in rugby league there is a team called North Sydney. Footyheads call them 'Norths'. However, if you are in aussie rules territory and you are talking about North Melbourne, you would say 'North', without the 's' on the end. It might sound like a minor point to you, but if you have the wrong ending, on the wrong word, in the wrong territory, you might as well give the game away now!

Names also fit into this category. It's kind of cool, and very Australian, to add an 'o' or an 'ie' to the end of every surname. But, again, be warned! If you get the wrong ending you will sound like a real out-of-towner. The surname Wilkins, for example, becomes Wilko, not Wilkie. However, a surname like Longman can be either Longo, or Longie. The only way you can be assured is to listen carefully to footyheads more advanced than you.

One of the early mistakes I made with soccer was to say, *'He head-butted the ball in for a goal!'* How red did I go? I felt like a beetroot. Any footyhead worth his or her salt knows that you don't 'head-butt' a ball, you simply 'head' it.

If you want to fit in immediately, pick on the ref, but before that, a quick lesson in sports psychology...

Lingo for the referee/umpire

Firstly, referees are those in charge of soccer, rugby league and rugby union games. In aussie rules, umpires are in charge. While there is very little difference it could be argued that a referee is the authority in a game of football while an umpire is only there to interpret the laws of the game when required by the players, which is why aussie rules is the most free-flowing game of all four codes of football. For our purpose here, I'll refer to all of them as referees.

Referees tend to have egos the same size as (if not bigger than) your average football star. They are always right. They like to be in control and therefore have an incredible understanding of the game's rules and how players try to break them.

Remember this: every time you shout abuse at the referee you will be spurring him on to greater heights of egomania. Refs love it when you tell them they've made a mistake because they *know* they couldn't possibly have! They take great pride in listening to you screaming 'rubbish!' from the sideline. They feel sorry for you because they realise you are merely taking out all of your weekly anxieties from work, or home-related stress on them. What I'm saying is, don't feel bad about doing it – they expect it and enjoy it!

On the whole, referees should be given credit for the job they do – they are another spoke in the wheel and without them, the game couldn't continue. So by all means, shout at them, but shout with respect!

Some referee-specific lingo from the crowd:

'You've got to be joking!'
'Get off, you bludger!'
'C'mon ref, you couldn't control a Z-grade game!'
'Get a life!'
'Why don't you get a guide dog – you're obviously blind!'

Once the referee is reduced to a blubbering mess on the side-line, too scared to blow his whistle again in case you throttle him, it might be time to turn your attention to the players.

Lingo for the teams

Learn to recognise faults in the opposition's game. Bag them mercilessly every time they drop a ball or miss a tackle. Often you will find members of your team making the same mistakes – ignore these. Pretend they never happened.

Just as you boo the ref any time he's within hearing distance, try the same tactics on visiting team players. Your mission is to distract them. Get them off guard. Frighten them with the wisdom of your knowledge of the game. Try some of these lines for starters:

'Go home – you're a joke!'
'How did you get picked, you Wally!'
'Careful, pretty boy, you might get hurt.'
'Ah, you're nothing but a bunch of Nevilles!'

(A *Neville* is a nobody. It was made popular by former Queensland rugby league player, current Queensland coach and football commentator Paul 'Fatty' Vautin, although Australian coach, Bob Fulton, could lay claim to inventing the term.)

While it's important for you to harass the visiting team, remember to also come up with a few positive lines each time your team is within earshot. Motivational lines like:

'Smash 'em!'
'C'mon, all the way!'
'You're all over them – now score!'

At the end of the day, if you've put in the hard yards (*see glossary*) as a spectator you can feel proud of your team's win. Alternatively, if your side lost, you must accept some of the responsibility – you just didn't work hard enough to get the other team off edge.

Learning from media commentators

Aside from listening to the regulars in a football crowd, the best way to pick up the local lingo and the in-phrases is to listen carefully to radio and TV commentators.

RUGBY LEAGUE FAN: CAROLYN HARRIGAN

Carolyn Harrigan is married to rugby league's highest profile referee. During 1995 the Harrigan family went on a football roller-coaster ride – the highpoint being Bill's appointment as a fulltime Superleague referee, the lowpoint being his mid-season sacking from the rival Australian Rugby League and highly publicised ejection from the home ground of an ARL loyal team.

Carolyn believes, despite it being a tough year, the seeds of prosperity have been sown: 'The whole Superleague issue was very exciting when it was first announced. But with the split of loyalties between Superleague and the ARL a lot of friendships have been strained, if not broken, even in refereeing circles.

'At least we are guaranteed a better family life now. Bill used to referee all weekend as well as working fulltime. The other benefit of Superleague is that we will have the competition draw months in advance – previously, we had to wait till Thursday nights to find out where Bill would be refereeing on the weekend. It could have been anywhere – Auckland, Perth, Townsville – you name it.'

Carolyn admits she knew nothing about football when she first met Bill ten years ago and despite having one of the best teachers available, she still can't claim to be any expert.

'Bill and I were both police officers. I first saw him at a police rugby game and then met him at a rugby league Grand Final that he was refereeing and I was patrolling. My non-existent knowledge of football picked up a lot after that because I had no choice! I even got hold of a copy of the rulebook once, but that didn't really do me any good.

'In the early days when we started going out he used to sit down and dissect each game of rugby league. I felt like I had to get in on the action and learn a bit. But being married to a referee you really don't get to follow any particular team so it's more difficult to build up an interest. There isn't really any social scene for referees and their families, either, because they're all off in different directions each week, so you never catch up.

'We don't have much to do with the players' wives because we don't go back to the club after the game. We're outcasts really,' Carolyn says with a laugh.

'You even get abused walking out of a ground – people generally mutter something as you go by. But in the grandstand I hear people abusing Bill constantly and it really used to worry me. I'd turn around and give them the old filthy look routine.

'Now I just sit there, watch Bill proudly and try to remain pretty inconspicuous, but the kids sometimes yell out, "That's my Dad!" Then they wave at him and call out. They're only kids, they don't know about the politics of sport yet.'

Fashionable ways of describing players' moves and tactics can all be picked up from the media, because, let's face it, these guys and girls are at the heart of it every working moment! It's not just run-of-the-mill stuff either, it's the real hard-core lingo like 'home ground advantage'. If people hear you using such terminology they will immediately think you are a true-blue footyhead.

A 'home ground advantage' means that the team playing with the support of the crowd has an obvious edge over the visiting team. Believe it or not, the worth of a home advantage varies from ground to ground because of design. The accoustics at a ground surrounded by grandstands will be much better, highlighting any noise and making it sound much more dramatic. A ground with only one grandstand and open space everywhere else lets the sound dissipate, so the cheering loses its impact.

Grounds like the MCG in Victoria, Ellis Park in South Africa and the Maracana Stadium in Brazil can be described as having '20 point advantages', meaning that the home side might as well start the game 20 points in front because of the fear a crowd can instill in the home team's opponents.

Sports psychologists actually teach sportsmen and women how to either ignore a negative crowd or use it to their advantage. When a footy team runs out onto the ground you will see players using different techniques to adjust to the atmosphere.

Some will stand quietly by the sideline and slowly pan around the ground, taking it all in like an army general at war, treating the crowd as the enemy and planning to be victorious over all. Others barely recognise there is a crowd there at all and seem so focussed on their mission that they look right through it, concentrating only on their inner strength.

Crowd behaviour also varies between sports and between

countries. Tennis crowds are expected to remain silent while a point is being played, but basketball crowds are expected to make as much noise as possible to distract the home team's opponents. Each time the visiting team gets within scoring range the band clatters and clangs, the crowd yells and screams and unless the shooter is totally focussed on the hoop, he or she is likely to miss the shot.

Internationally, South American crowds like to play music and dance in the stands, English soccer crowds are thought to have a violent bent and love confrontation, while the good old Aussie crowd is pretty much there to have a good time. Remember though, there will be exceptions to every rule.

PLAYER RESEARCH

Before a game gets underway or during various stops in play you will no doubt get into fairly heavy conversation with the people sitting around you. You will find that most crowds are like a collection of little choirs – in each group there will be a conductor who rallies those around him/her into shouting the right things. Believe me, if you plan on going along to a game without reducing yourself to a screaming maniac, you are kidding yourself.

Being part of a crowd is being part of that choir. You need to sing in tune. The woman next to you screams, you join in. The bloke behind you calls the referee a ponce, everyone around him agrees. So forget the 'not me' act: you will surprise yourself by being caught up in it all. Once you get over the shock of being 'one of them' you will laugh at yourself (the way you used to laugh at others) and then you'll really start getting involved. You will love it.

Now, if you are going to behave like an intelligent member of a footy crowd, you must educate yourself adequately.

When a break in play occurs, those sitting around you will want to get to know you better since you've agreed with everything they've shouted throughout the game. This is where the study comes in. Don't be afraid, no huffing and puffing please, this can be enjoyable too.

The person sitting next to you is likely to:

a. Crack a tinny from the esky (if you are sitting on the hill)
b. Pour a coffee from the thermos (if you are in a stand)
c. Sip another chardonnay (if you are in a private box)

Then they will start a conversation in one of two ways...

1. The gentle approach

Footyhead: *'The bloody ref hasn't got a clue, has he?'*
Response: Agree. Then add an observation of your own such as *'unbelievable'.*

Now that you've established you are both sitting on the same side of the fence your newfound friend will want to know some of your views. The best way to sound up-to-date, intelligent, and a master of the game is to get in first. Don't wait for a question that you might not be able to answer. This is where homework comes in.

Say you've been studying the goal kicker for your team, Dwayne Bruce. If he's kicked three out of three in the first half you will be able to say, quite authoritatively, ***'Gee, Brucey's putting them away this week, isn't he?'*** Always finish your statements with a question – it's part of footyhead talk. Conversely, if he's missed three out of three you can shake your head in despair and claim, ***'Brucey's had a shocker, hasn't he?'*** Your colleague will be impressed. The rest of the halftime break will be spent sharing such insights.

2. The attacking style

Footyhead: *'What would you know about a game of footy?'*
Response: Don't get edgy and start thinking the bloke knows that you're a novice – tell him the truth about it being your first game but disguise it. For example, *'Mate, I've been following it all my life but this is the first Saturday I've ever had off and I tell you, being here is so much better than watching it on telly, isn't it?'*

Again, the question at the end of your statement throws the ball back into his court and he has to come up with the next line of conversation.

Because you sound so positive your friend will have immediate sympathy for you and probably start telling you of all the great games he's seen during his life. You can throw in the appropriate sound effects such as 'wow', 'fair dinkum, eh?' and 'I would love to have seen that one!'

Let's take stock. You've survived the first half, you've made it through the halftime break sounding like a legend and you've got a new buddy. This means you can feel right at home during the second half and start shouting with even more passion than before.

When fulltime is signalled (by a referee's whistle, a siren or a hooter) you will be a fully fledged footyhead.

How unreal does that sound!

HOW TO FALL IN LOVE WITH FOOTY

All of us are interested in something – art, politics, the environment, law or just plain personalities. Football has all of it. Only recently, at a special function celebrating the wit, wisdom and candour of some of Australia's greatest thinkers, one of these supposed great minds declared, 'I remember when the only thing to do on Saturdays was to go to the boring old footy!'

Immediately that person was crossed off the list of great thinkers. How could anybody be so naive? How could anybody ever describe it as 'boring old footy'?! Have you ever heard anyone say, 'Oh, it's just boring old art' or 'It's just boring old literature'? No. Not even a footyhead would say that, because despite popular opinion, footyheads aren't naive. They may not all be able to recite Shakespeare or identify the works of the great Impressionists, but they do know that art and literature are valuable components of society just like football.

Some cynics may suggest that while art and literature are valuable, sport is not. People who subscribe to that line of thinking are more than cynical; they are stupid. And there is usually only one reason for that – they failed at school sport. Often it's not their own fault: often it's because there was nobody around to show them exactly how to catch a basketball or kick a football or hit a softball. Anyone who hasn't experienced the pure joy of hand-eye co-ordination at work has missed out on one of the great thrills in life. Go and watch the kids playing in the school yard or in the park across the road. They are in heaven – they're showing off to their mates about how high or far they can kick a ball . . . or displaying pinpoint accuracy in shooting baskets . . . they are getting hot and sweaty . . . their hearts are pounding . . . they feel fit . . . they want more . . . they are in love with life. That's what sport does to you.

Now why don't you run across the road and tell them you are Tony Lockett's cousin or Mal Meninga's sister and ask if you can join in. Tell them you played soccer with Pele once and he'll be round for dinner next week. You'll have those kids knocking your door down every afternoon asking you to go and play with them.

Go and experience how thrilling it is when you finally get some distance and air under the ball you kick and it goes straight between those twigs that have been put up as goalposts. You watch – you'll shout and scream like any of the other World Cup stars, waiting for your team mates to run up and jump on you, for the crowd to erupt into a standing ovation and for the photographers to start flashing their bulbs.

Then you'll remember you're in the park across the road, with only the neighbours looking sideways at you through their narrowly opened doors. Don't feel strange. Recognise their perverted stares as plain old jealousy. They wish they were out there sharing the joy of life too.

If it's as good as that with a bunch of seven-year-olds, can you imagine what it must be like out there in the international arena with a sellout crowd of 100,000 and another billion or so watching you around the world on pay TV? Awesome.

The benefits of sport aren't just psychological, either. Take a look at some of the results found in an Australian Sports Commission report.

STARS

TONY LOCKETT is one of aussie rules' most talented forwards, whose goal-kicking ability is sought after far and wide.

MAL MENINGA was one of Australia's most impressive rugby league captains ever, during the '80s and '90s. He is now an administrator of the game.

PELE is the greatest soccer player of all time. He rose out of the slums of Brazil to international stardom through his skills with the boot.

Australian Sports Commission Report

■ Sixty-five percent of the urban population participate as spectators of sport and 96% of people watch sport at some stage on television.

■ In 1990-91 the Australian government outlaid $13.2 billion for health rectification and $485.4 million for research, preventative activities and health promotion programs. If more Australians actually PARTICIPATED in sport the cost of our Federal Health Budget would be drastically reduced.

■ An estimated 40,000 work-related back injuries each year in Australia costs the country $600 million in compensation and 190 million lost working days. Sixty-eight percent of people with back problems do NO exercise or exercise at very low levels.

■ More than 111,000 people are employed in the sports industry while each year approximately 10,000 sports people enter Australia for competition. (This figure will rise drastically between now and the 2000 Olympics.)

■ A conservative estimate of the amount of money spent in Australia by tourists who participate in sport while they are here is in excess of $1,900 million.

■ In one year alone more than $185 million worth of manufactured sporting goods were turned over.

■ Wages and salaries in the sporting goods manufacturing sector totalled $36.5 million.

■ Approximately 13,000 jobs in manufacturing and commerce are attributable to sport.

SOURCE: Sport – A Great Investment, *Australian Sports Commission 1993*

Back to the arty argument (in case you aren't yet convinced). Art and literature can be used to trace the history of mankind. So too can sport. Art and literature can be used to compare societies. So too can sport. Art and literature can teach you to broaden your way of thinking. So too can sport. Art and literature bring enjoyment to millions. So too can sport. But can you show me a piece of art or literature that unites a nation? Sport can. And what of the economic worth? Or the physical, emotional and social value? Sport, sport and more sport. Did you know that sport is Australia's largest industry? Did you know that in one year $261 million was spent on heart surgery in Australia, and 98% of the recipients played no sport or partook of no physical activity? If we all enjoyed sport, think of how much money we could save!

It doesn't mean we all have to rush out and try to become the next Pele or Mal Meninga – just as we can't all paint like the great Renoir. But we can all enjoy sport, just as we enjoy art, and that's good for the soul.

Our whole way of thinking in Australia needs to be challenged. There seems to be a constant battle here between sport and the arts. Throughout Europe, sport is considered an art and society studies sportspeople just as they study dancers – as performers on a stage. I don't mean that if our footballers all put tights on they'd look like Nureyev, but you go and watch a slow motion replay of Laurie Daley ducking and weaving through a pack of opponents. Watch the muscles and strength on display, his ability to read the game as it unfolds and stay a step ahead of all the others as he dives over the try line. That is art. Buy a ticket to the MCG next time Gary Ablett plays there and watch him approach the goal posts at a million miles an hour with opponents swarming all over him...watch the mental lines he draws between his hands, his feet, the ball and the goal and then watch as he paints the picture to perfection. That is art.

So how do you fall in love with footy, you ask? Just the way you fall in love with a man. Look for something you like. Look for the right shape, the right coloured hair, the right dress sense. Look for the footy player with the right style, one who is speeding down the wing or is brutal in his tackles. Listen to how he talks in interviews, watch the way he saunters out onto the field and the effects he has on his opponents. Watch the way he warms up. You'll soon fall in love with the game he plays.

If men aren't your scene, look for something that is: soak up the atmosphere, spot the fashion gurus in the crowd or check out the referees' power-play. Remember, the sports field is a subplot of life: it's just a smaller version of everything else that is going on in the world – relationships, politics, medicine, fashion, law. It's all happening on the footy oval, and to top it all off, it's mostly environmentally friendly.

Guess what? You've graduated to the next level. Let's take a closer look at the individual codes.

3

SOCCER

A QUICK HISTORY LESSON

Soccer is where it all began. Before man handled a ball, he kicked it. Stories have been gathered from the ancient Romans, Greeks, and Chinese about early forms of football.

It should be pointed out now that Australia is one of only a handful of countries that calls the game 'soccer'. Throughout Europe, Latin America and Africa soccer is considered the only kind of football, and so that is what it's called. There are pockets of rugby union in these regions, for instance Argentina, France and South Africa are all strong rugby nations, but the term 'football' is reserved for soccer.

Early on we recounted how the Normans used to decapitate their foes and kick the heads through the streets as a kind of victory celebration. Other legends speak of fertility rituals where round discs representing the sun and the moon were kicked across grounds running from east to west. In some lands an animal's head was used as a football and the winning team got to bury the head on their lands ensuring a fruitful season. (I'm glad we don't play that variety of soccer these days!)

Soccer's success came and went in waves. At one stage it was deemed a threat to national security in England because all the boys and men were playing it rather than practising their skills with bows and arrows. Imprisonment was threatened for anybody participating in such games of 'no value'. Back then the game was played using the entire village as the ground and up to 500 men as players. A ball would be kicked from one end of town to the other with broken doors, broken legs and sometimes death the result. In 1314 King Edward II issued a declaration banning the game. It was described as 'nothing but beastly fury and extreme violence'. Some would say the description is still rather apt.

But they say you can't keep a good man down, and neither can you keep a good game down. English soccer clubs were formed in the early 1800s, and played with various rules depending on which part of the country you were from. Once players from around the nation came together in universities, such as Cambridge, the first unified rules of the game were put in place.

A meeting was held in 1863 at the Freemasons' Tavern in London and the Football Association was formed. One of the greatest competitions played today is the Football Association Cup, known as the FA Cup, which is contested by English teams and followed worldwide.

The biggest, most prestigious and glamorous footballing feast, though, is the World Cup. Held once every four years, teams from right around the globe battle through a series of qualifying rounds for one of only 32 berths, and coverage of the tournament rivals the Olympics as the most watched event on the planet. Australia has made it to the World Cup only once – back in 1974 when we were eliminated after the first round. Australia's history in soccer dates back to the 1880s, but it struggled for widespread recognition until mass European immigration after World War II increased the demand for the game.

With changing qualifying rules on the international scene, Australia's chances of reaching future World Cup finals have been made easier. Success there would add to our top form in women's soccer, Olympic soccer and junior soccer, where we are ranked amongst the world's top teams.

FACT

History was made at the 1995 World Youth Soccer Championships in Qatar. In a game between the teams of Honduras and the Netherlands, Honduras had used all three substitutes, had four players sent off through bad behaviour and when another player had to be carried off injured with the score at 7-1 in favour of the Dutch, the match had to be abandoned because the Central Americans no longer had the required minimum number of seven players on the field!

WHAT THE GAME IS ALL ABOUT

Soccer is about being an outdoor performer. Who wants to be pent up on a tiny, dark, indoor stage when you can be outside breathing in the air of life and performing to hundreds of thousands of screaming fans at one time? Being a star of the stage is rather quaint, being a star of the footy field is big time!

Soccer players are experts at all the arts: they can sing (anything except the national anthem in most cases), dance and act with all the panache in the world.

Basically, the game is one of the simplest you'll find – you must kick a ball into the opponents' goal in order to score. That's it. In fact, because the rules of soccer are so simple, many other sports have been based on it. Waterpolo used to be called water soccer, for instance. One of the latest sports developed is called snowball, a variation of soccer played on the snow-covered fields of Russia.

THE PLAYERS

GOALIES: There are 11 players per team and only one is allowed to use his hands. The goal keeper, or goalie, is the one who always wears outrageous colours, often has long flowing hair, wears hefty padded gloves and loves to dive – even when it's not entirely necessary.

Goalies are heroes because once the pressure's on they are charged with the job of stopping the opponents from scoring – they are the last line of defence. If you are colour blind or have

LYDIA DOWSE: GENERAL MANAGER, UTS SYDNEY OLYMPIC

Lydia Dowse broke with all tradition in 1995 when she was appointed general manager of UTS Sydney Olympic, in Soccer Australia's national league competition. She is one of the first women to hold such a post, and she is Anglo-Australian in a predominantly Greek club.

'Soccer Australia has taken a new, innovative direction with the game in this country. The whole face of soccer is changing. Our traditional Greek supporters have been saying they've never seen so many anglo-Australians, so many Asians, and so many families coming to the games – so soccer's base is broadening and our audiences are starting to reflect the diverse make-up of our culture.

'Judging by a team's performance on the ground, you can tell a lot about what's going on behind the scenes in a club. Our management and directorship have achieved a closer relationship with the players in the last year, and it's reflected in our growing crowds which are up three-and four-fold in one season.

'We aren't just breaking down cultural barriers but also the rivalry between football codes. During 1995 we started working closely with our local rugby league team for marketing purposes. We might even start sharing the same playing ground in the future. That's the direction sport is going these days.

'It's been a bit of a shock for me, coming from a legal background into a sports management role. Being involved in a football club takes your heart, your soul, your family, your time – it becomes your whole life. Every ounce of commitment and energy is taken out of you. The fans have demands, the board of directors have demands, so too do the players and Soccer Australia, the governing body of the sport here. But don't get the wrong idea – I love what I do and those difficult times are far outweighed by the good times.

'Seeing all the ingredients come together to put your team on top of the ladder makes all of the hard times worthwhile!'

trouble distinguishing one player from the other, you can actually close your eyes and pick a goalie from sound only. Whenever they make a save (stop the other team from scoring) they start yelling at their team mates as if they're captain, coach and general all rolled into one. This is part of the acting job – in case anyone didn't see them make the save, they let you hear about it. Types

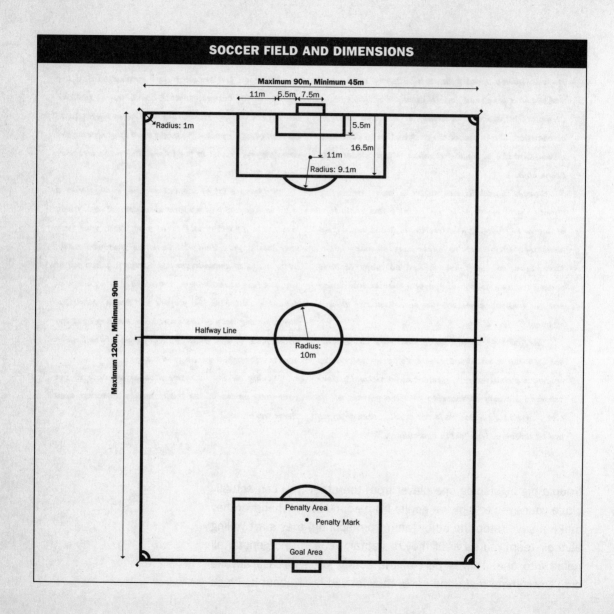

SOCCER FIELD AND DIMENSIONS

Maximum 90m, Minimum 45m

11m   5.5m   7.5m

Radius: 1m

5.5m

16.5m

11m

Radius: 9.1m

Maximum 120m, Minimum 90m

Halfway Line

Radius: 10m

Penalty Area

Penalty Mark

Goal Area

best suited for a role like this would include Arnold Schwarzenegger and Sylvester Stallone.

STRIKERS are the other heroes. Each team designates one or two strikers, depending on their 'game plan', which we'll discuss a little later. The strikers in the team are the ones who must, above all others, kick the goals. To become a striker a player needs a long history of A-grade acting along with incredible foot–eye co-ordination and reflexes to die for. Somebody like Gary Sweet would make a perfect striker if he ever took up soccer.

Strikers must love pressure and the limelight, because both are usually on them. They must be prepared for hundreds and thousands of adoring fans. You see, part of the striker's role is that whenever he kicks a goal he must collapse in front of the crowd, he must raise his hands to the heavens and thank God, he must burst into tears of emotion as if he's just witnessed a miracle, and then wait for his team mates to join in the celebration. Once this marvel of soccer has been performed, the striker makes his way back to his spot on the ground and gets on with the game nonchalantly. A rare talent indeed.

In fact, the International Football Federation (FIFA), which controls the game worldwide, even has a paragraph in its *Laws of the Game* dedicated entirely to the celebration of a goal:

After a goal has been scored, the player who has scored it is allowed to share his joy with his teammates. However, the referee must not allow them to spend an inordinate amount of time in their opponents' half of the field. Neither will he tolerate players dashing past the billboards or climbing up the crowd barriers. In either of these two cases, he will caution the offending player for ungentlemanly conduct.

The (in)famous French player, Eric Cantona, behaved in an 'ungentlemanly' manner during a game and hurdled the barrier to karate kick a vocal spectator. Cantona was given a couple of months forced holiday for his efforts.

It's strikers and goalkeepers who have the highest profiles, and deservedly so, because if a team wins, it's usually their prowess that has ensured it. If the team loses, on the other hand, they cop most of the flak. Theirs are upmarket, high-pressured jobs that deserve every bit of the attention they get, not to mention the millions of dollars they also get paid at international level.

The great Pele was a striker who wore jersey No.10 for Brazil and is deemed the greatest soccer player ever to have lived...he's one of the world's four most recognised people. The No.10 jumper is still the highest sought after commercially. It was also Pele that converted the USA to soccer, culminating in their successful hosting of the World Cup in 1994 (which, incidentally, Brazil won).

A SWEEPER is a player that patrols the backline. In other words, he's charged with plugging the gaps in defence and acting as a second-last resort (the goalkeeper being the last resort) to stop the opposition scoring. One of Australia's best current soccer players, Ned Zelic, is a sweeper worth millions on the international market.

Sweepers are like crows – they sit on their perch and observe the game from a different perspective, then move in for the kill at the appropriate moment. Because play continues straight on from their critical move to the next phase of the game, they rarely get the recognition they deserve from the crowd. After a striker has kicked a goal the world stops, and he's worshipped; after a goalie does his thing the crowd gasps and he's applauded; but when a sweeper steals the ball from the attacking team or prevents a goal from being scored, play simply continues and he's forgotten in the rush of things.

A sweeper also has a roving licence, to move forward at his discretion in order to orchestrate an attacking movement. He's a bit like a co-star, always in the action but never landing the lead role, or a behind-the-scenes type who doesn't need to be reminded constantly of his worth. Men with mystique suit sweeping positions – Clint Eastwood, Tom Cruise or Antonio Banderas would revel in the role if they could leave their egos at home.

Beyond these starring roles come the midfield players, central defenders and wide running players who perform along the lines of wingers in rugby league – they storm down the outside and try to set up scoring positions for their team mates to capitalise on.

WINGERS, as the name suggests, are positioned on either side of the field patrolling the touchline, or sideline. The role is interchangeable with that of a **MIDFIELDER**, who can be positioned on the touchline also. (See diagram of field positions.) Speed and accuracy are the most vital skills for wingers.

MIDFIELDERS fall into three specific zones – central midfield, right midfield and left midfield. Along with wingers, midfielders require plenty of stamina as they race from one end of the ground to the other. They are never too far from the action. Keeping with our Hollywood comparisons, stunt-men and high-powered performers like Evil Knevel would make the best wingers and midfielders.

FULLBACKS have three specialised positions – centreback, left back and right back. These three patrol the goal area and provide a buffer zone between the attacking team and the goal keeper. Mafia types would love these positions because of the demand for tight security.

Throw-in

FIELD POSITIONS

The diagram of field positions shows two teams, playing with different formations. The team marked with an '▲' is the current formation used by the Australian men's team, under coach Eddie Thomson. It's called a 4-4-2: 4 players in the backline, 4 in centre field and 2 up front.

The team marked '△' is playing with a 4-3-3 formation, favoured by some European countries: 4 players in the backline, 3 in centre field, and three in the front line.

Coaches, captains, and sometimes the entire team, work together in devising formations for specific games. Depending on the talent available on playing day, and the type of opposition the team will be facing, the 'winning formula' is constructed. Sometimes formations change in the course of a game – depending on the state of play. If at half-time team ▲ is three goals ahead, they may opt for a more defensive formation for the second half, to ensure team △ doesn't score. If team ▲ is three goals behind at half-time, the formation will be altered for a more attacking game.

COACHES

The coach of a soccer team can't be mentioned in the same breath as any of the players. These people are gods. They speak from the heavens, mouthing abstract messages for the team to ponder. They also manage to swing from job to job like orangutans at the local zoo. The only coach who keeps his job at the end of the year is the one whose club finishes first. Even then he's lucky. All other coaches jump onto the soccer roundabout and try to jump off at the nearest lucrative intersection.

As in all roles, there's a scale of coaches too – from club level

FIELD POSITIONS

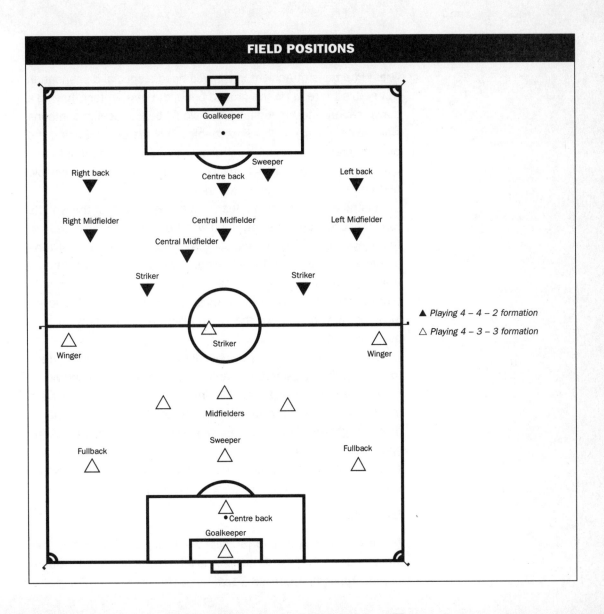

▲ Playing 4 – 4 – 2 formation
△ Playing 4 – 3 – 3 formation

through to national level. Coaches at national level can't be approached by normal citizens like you and me. They are like the Great Pharoahs of Ancient Egypt. You need a special dispensation to be able to tread on the ground beneath them. In fact, having a conversation with a national coach would be like seeing someone walking on water – highly improbable. Only the chosen ones, the players, are so privileged. Australia, thankfully, doesn't fit into this category, yet. Our national coaches are still highly approachable and appreciate all the attention they can get.

Australia's senior men's team isn't listed amongst the world's top 50 soccer countries yet. But it won't be long. Our junior teams, the Joeys (under 17), Young Socceroos (under 20), and Olyroos (under 23) – are ranked in the world's top five and our women's team, the Matildas, is inside the top eight. Once our senior men's team reaches similar levels I imagine our coaches will also be elevated, hovering above the ground like sacred icons waiting to be worshipped.

Coaches are employed by clubs, or by state and national bodies, to devise winning game plans and to convert a group of individual players into one strong team playing as a united force. Coaches must work with the difficult combination of skill and personality in order to get the best from each player. Aside from game day speeches, the coach is responsible for coordinating training programs for the team, and may be involved in off-field activities such as attending social functions or making guest appearances.

THE BALL

This is one of the major differences between soccer and the other three codes of footy. A soccer ball is perfectly round, with a circumference between 68-71cm.

SOCCER FAN: VALERIE WADE

It's easy to get carried away with the glamour and big bucks of an international game like soccer but behind the scenes there are still all the usual problems – finding a place to live, making new friends, and helping the kids settle into another new environment.

Socceroo captain Paul Wade and his wife Valerie moved their family out of sociable Melbourne to take on the daunting task of captaining the new Canberra Cosmos team in Soccer's 'A' League during 1995.

'I actually met Paul at the soccer. I used to follow it from a very young age and I'd go to games with my dad. I wanted to play when I was little but my dad wouldn't let me because it wasn't the done thing for girls back then.

'You don't have to be brought up on the game to fall in love with it. I mean nobody has a greater passion for the game than Paul – he loves it more than anything – yes, including me! If you meet somebody like that you can't help but fall in love with the game too. It's easy to get involved when there's somebody that you can follow the game with.

'In Melbourne, soccer has a wonderful social scene – all the wives and girlfriends would go to the games and we'd all go out to dinner with the guys afterwards but, of course, it's a new and different scene in Canberra. Every time you move it takes a little while to re-establish yourself as a family.'

Soccer's heritage in Australia is based largely around our ethnic population and with most clubs you will be mixing with different cultures.

'In Canberra there is a strong Croatian base. As a wife I'm on my own a bit, because it's not the done thing for their wives to come to the games. If the girls do come to the game they go home afterwards while all the men go out together.'

On a national basis, the Australian Soccer team probably spends more time overseas than any of our other football codes. This sounds great, but it carries a fair deal of stress.

'Coaches don't like the wives travelling with the players because they say we are a distraction. You can't stay with your man anyway. You stay in separate hotels, you only get to see them for ten minutes here or there and all you can do is watch them play the game...you really can't enjoy a place unless you're sharing it with somebody else.

'Even just moving from club to club takes its toll, so you need to stay optimistic. You have to decide that you are going to enjoy a place before you get there, otherwise you'd have no chance of survival. So, we do enjoy it. We actually love it!'

The ground is divided into thirds – the front, middle and back thirds. The front third is where the strikers shoot for goal, the middle third is the battle zone for midfielders and the back third is where the goalie and the backline do their thing.

The usual coin toss is conducted by the ref with the winning skipper given an ultimatum: choose the end of the ground you wish to defend or choose to kick off! This is one of the nice things about soccer: both teams come away from the coin toss as winners.

For the next 90 minutes you'll be watching a remarkable display of what man has done best since we arrived from *Planet of the Apes* – kick, dribble and shoot. Even from the opening minutes you'll start to pick the personalities in the team simply from the way they play the game.

OFFSIDE

Fred Funk is a midfielder who spends most of his time hiding behind team mates. He is the guy who doesn't work too hard in training unless the coach is watching him. He's the one who lies awake at night dreaming of being the hero in the game without actually having to do any of the work. Fred's also a conspiracy theorist. He believes the only reason the media don't focus on him after the game is that he's suffering from the tall poppy syndrome. He thinks he's so good that the other players are jealous and have convinced the media not to talk to him.

Because of Fred's total lack of concentration he often finds himself in an offside position. Not having studied the rules of the game, Fred doesn't realise how complicated the offside rule is and continues to fall into the same trap week after week.

Basically, there must be at least two opponents between a player and the opposition's goal. If there is only one opponent, for example the goalie, then the attacking player is offside. If Fred would only realise that he needs two players between himself and the goal he might be able to do something useful for a change – like score a goal!

Nobody can explain the entire offside rule in plain English, so it's time to go straight to the FIFA *Laws of the Game*:

1. *A player is in an offside position if he is nearer to his opponents' goal-line than the ball, unless:*
   (a) he is in his own half of the field of play, or
   (b) he is not nearer to his opponents' goal-line than
      at least two of his opponents.

2. *A player shall only be declared offside and penalised for being so, if, at the moment the ball touches, or is played by, one of his team, he is, in the opinion of the referee:*
   (a) interfering with play or with an opponent, or
   (b) seeking to gain an advantage by being in that position.

3. *A player shall not be declared offside by the referee:*
   (a) merely because of his being in an offside position, or
   (b) if he receives the ball directly from a goal-kick, a corner kick or a throw in.

Something obviously got lost in the translation. If you can work out the above explanation you are probably more advanced than

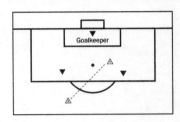

Offside
Player 'Y' is offside because there is only one, instead of at least two opponents, between him and the goal

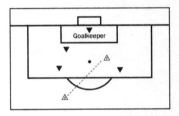

Onside
Player 'Y' is now onside because there are two opponents between him and the goal line.

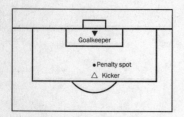

Penalty kick

If a serious offence is committed in the penalty area, a penalty kick can be given. Only the goalkeeper is permitted to defend the goal mouth.

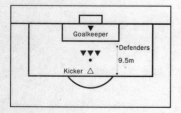

Direct free kick

If a direct free kick is awarded, any number of opponents can stand in front of their goal mouth to block an attempt at goal.

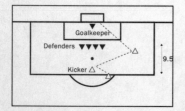

Indirect free kick

An indirect free kick is for lesser penalties and the ball must be touched by at least one other player before it can be kicked at goal.

90% of the world's soccer players, who continue to argue over the interpretation of the offside rule.

Let's move on shall we, time is ticking away...

FREE KICKS

Tom Terrific is the maniac who runs up and down the sideline for the duration of the match and never has the ball for more than a split second before finding the gap in defence and sending a team mate through for a goal. Although he makes most of his team's goals possible, Tom never expects the limelight. However, the striker on his team has gone over on his ankle and Tom is asked to take the free kick after his side is given a penalty.

Penalties are awarded against teams for breaking the rules and abusive behaviour. There are three types of free kicks: Penalty, Direct and Indirect.

After the game, when the lights are flashing and the microphones are buzzing as the sideline commentators give their observations, Tom Terrific is already showered, dressed and ready to take his wife and six kids to the movies, despite the fact he was successful in all three attempts he made at goal.

He's the first to arrive at training the next day, and once the coach calls it quits for the afternoon, Tom hangs around and does another squillion sit-ups on his own, in the dark.

RED AND YELLOW CARDS

Danny Drama rarely touches the ball. He just positions himself somewhere visible and shouts useless tips to his team mates, who are too busy to hear him. Despite the fact that his foot never comes into contact with the ball, he's got all the right moves – he'll spend his time kicking the ground whenever a shot goes astray, he'll punch the air with his fists as though he made every goal possible and during breaks in play he'll check out his dreadlocks in the little mirror he keeps in the pocket of his shorts. Danny's mirror often comes in handy, though: he can use it to flash the sun's reflection into the eyes of his opponents, blinding them momentarily and creating a possible scoring opportunity for his team mates.

Unfortunately, Danny shone the light into the ref's eyes and he's been found out. As a result, the opposition gets a direct free kick and Danny is red-carded, meaning he is sent off, leaving his team one man down. A player who has been shown a red card cannot be replaced, unlike an injured player who leaves the ground.

The referee carries two cards into every game – a yellow one and a red one. The yellow card is a cautionary card, used to put players on notice for misconduct. The referee will blow his whistle, hold the yellow card up to the player, and then to the official scorers. If the player continues to act-up, the ref is entitled to bring out the red card.

RED CARDS

- *Abusive language*
- *Violent play*
- *Committing a foul after being yellow-carded*

YELLOW CARDS

- *Tripping*
- *Stalling*
- *Arguing*

SPECIAL SKILLS

Tireless Tim is the everywhere man. An opponent needs to be tackled? Tireless is there. A team mate needs support on the touchline? He's there as well. The goalie needs backup when a corner kick is on? Tim's your man. But by halftime the coach needs to sub him off because he's hyperventilated and having a seizure. As soon as he can breathe again and his concussed head is bandaged up, he's subbed straight back for more of the same.

Tireless Tim has the crowds oohing and aahing with his display of ball control. He can dribble, tapping the ball from one foot to the other as he runs up field, dodging waiting opponents. He changes direction, uses the outside of his foot then the inside, and he throws his marker off by faking a shot to a team mate on his left before passing to someone on his right.

A stray kick from an opponent gives Tim the chance to head the ball upfield, towards his striker who's perfectly positioned for a goal. After some effective tackles, he gains possession of the ball and shows how he can kick – he puts in a volley, then a swerve ball, now a low drive, next a chip and, of course, the big one – a shot at goal!

Dribble

Dribbling is one of the most basic soccer skills but is highly impressive at elite level. Using the inside and outside of both feet, a skilled soccer player can make his legs look like elastic as he runs up field juggling the ball from one side to the other and throwing his opponents off course.

An extension of dribbling is the players' ability to use the rest of his body to keep control of the ball. Leaning, or feinting, provides the illusion of going one way while his feet might be going the other. Any little trick to fool, or bamboozle, the opponents will be advantageous.

Tackling

Unlike other codes of football, where the players are tackled, in soccer only the ball can be tackled. Players must try to wrestle the ball free from opponents using either a block tackle or a slide tackle.

BLOCK TACKLE: A successful block tackle effectively steals the ball from an opponent. The player not in possession will get his feet in between the ball and the opponent's feet and wrestle it free.

SLIDE TACKLE: A slide tackle is achieved by sliding towards the opponent in possession, to try and kick the ball free.

Tackling in soccer is highly skilful and fairly aggressive. Some dirty players opt to kick an opponent's legs, rather than the ball, so that when he collapses in agony the ball is free. Don't be fooled, though, by those Academy award winners who collapse the minute an opponent challenges for the ball. These actors are waiting for a free kick to be awarded for dangerous play but the referees are awake to this little trick and rarely award them in such situations.

Heading the ball

While players can't use their hands to pass the ball in soccer, they can certainly use their heads – physically as well as mentally.

Good distance and accuracy can be achieved by players who use their forehead to project the ball up or down field. Experienced players use their whole body and push themselves up to meet the approaching ball. Headers are used in general play and can also be used as a shot at goal.

Kicks

CHIP SHOT: The chip shot is a quick, sharp high kick using backspin and is useful in going over the top of an opponent or gaining some quick territory.

SWERVE BALL: The swerve ball is used in direct free kicks to get around the line of defenders. By kicking the ball with the side of the foot, rather than the front of the foot, the ball will spin into an arc.

VOLLEY: A volley is a kick made while the ball is still in the air.

WHO WAS THAT MAN?

In my first week at the ABC as a trainee sports commentator I was rostered on to cover the World Cup Soccer qualifying game between Australia and Israel at the Sydney Football Stadium. It was April 1989 and my supervising commentator was Peter Wilkins – a very experienced footyhead.

I was thoroughly enjoying myself sitting at the back of the commentary box when 'Wilko', continuing to give live commentary, handed me a microphone and a tape recorder and signalled for me to go down to the sideline.

My heart stopped when the ref blew the whistle to end game and I heard Wilko say on national radio: 'Now let's go down to the sideline with Tracey Holmes . . .'

The field was in turmoil. The ref had blown the whistle early and the Aussies were complaining that they'd been robbed of time. The score was 1-1 but because Israel's goal was an away goal it was worth two points and meant they progressed to the next round, effectively eliminating Australia from the World Cup. Four hundred photographers and TV crews from around the world had run onto the field to capture the emotion. I realised that ABC listeners were waiting for the same sort of action and it was up to me to deliver it.

There were no players within about a 50 metre radius from me and I couldn't get any closer to them because a television crewman was standing on my microphone lead and I couldn't budge. I saw a fuzzy, redheaded player in an Aussie jersey running in my direction so I shouted 'Hey, you, come here'. As he approached I whispered, with one hand over my microphone, 'Who are you?'

'Graham Arnold.'

Taking my shielding hand away from the microphone I nervously proclaimed 'Graham Arnold, you're going live around Australia on the ABC, what a traumatic game . . .'

He kindly answered all four of my stammering questions and I hastily crossed back to Wilko in the commentary box. I realised at that moment that if I was going to parade around the world's best sporting grounds as a commentator, I'd better learn what the game and the players were all about.

No need to say Graham Arnold has been a favourite of mine ever since. Not once at the many games and press conferences I have since seen him at has he ever reminded me of my naive, pathetic, inaugural performance. This book is designed to save YOU ever having to suffer the same kind of embarrassment.

The beautiful thing is, it's so easy! I only knew one player in the whole world of soccer – Graham Arnold – but it gave me the key to the door. I learnt which position he played in, what number he wore, his style of play, his team mates, clubs he played for, how successful they were, etc. etc. It's an easy plan to follow and before you know it – you'll be an armchair expert too.

GOAL KEEPING

Sammy Suave is the Mr Cool of the team. He saunters up to his opponents, in his own penalty box, and brushes them away like flies. He lazily takes his leg back and boots so far down field that the ball almost goes straight into the opposition's goal. When his goal is being attacked he dives, he jumps, he punches the ball and he leaves the opposition angry in frustration. And for the entire match, he doesn't even raise a sweat. Sammy's wife is just as cool. While 80,000 berserk fans scream madly at Sammy's Midas touch, Lulu just keeps filing her nails from the stand – she's seen Sammy do this a million times before and really can't get too excited by it all. While all the men in the crowd are secretly wishing they had Sammy's style, and his wife, all the women sitting nearby wish they were Lulu . . . for both her nails and her talented husband.

After making a save by either diving, jumping or scooping the ball up, a goal keeper has the added pressure of analysing the state of play before distributing the ball to a team mate. A goalie will either kick deeply to a waiting winger, or throw (javelin style) to one of the backs. He can patrol anywhere inside his penalty box but is allowed a maximum of four steps before releasing the ball.

SUBSTITUTES

Lenny Legend is the guy who spends every game on the subs bench but later, in the club, relives the game as if he was the only guy on the field. Nothing more needs to be said about this dreamer.

Up to five extra players can be named 'on the bench' [see glossary] for each team, but in international matches only two substitutes can be made. In other games, providing both teams agree and the referee has been informed, up to five substitutions can be made. A goalkeeper substitution can be made on top of these providing he is designated a specialist/substitute keeper before the match begins.

Any player (including a goalie) sent from the field for acting above and beyond Academy Award level, will not be replaced. If a specialist player such as goalkeeper is sent off, the coach will usually pull another player off, such as a midfielder, and replace him with a specialist goalie, if he has one.

REFEREES

Soccer referees are masochists. Nobody in the world is more hated for doing their chosen profession than soccer referees. At national and international level they do a brilliant job. If you were asked to referee a game of 'Pick the Legend' between Patrick Swayze, Mel Gibson, Tom Cruise and eight of their mates, you'll understand what I mean when I say they are hated...you'd end up with very few friends by picking one of those legends above any of the others. The rest of the team would probably come at you with spears!

It's the power of referees that is so disliked by the soccer players. Refs treat international legends like absolute schoolboys. The fact that players sometimes act like four-year-olds is no excuse. Before a game starts it's the ref's duty, along with assistance from his linesmen, to inspect the studs on the players' boots. This act of humiliation is performed in the tunnel leading from the dressing rooms onto the field.

Although I've never seen a player penalised for it, refs are also supposed to ensure that players keep their jerseys tucked into their shorts and their socks pulled up! This is just another powerplay – a way of referees to stamp their authority on the game before any of the players start to think they can take control.

If your brother/boyfriend/husband/uncle is a soccer player, never admit to him that you know this next rule – it will send them burning red with embarrassment:

Players are permitted to wear visible undergarments ... they must, however, be the same colour as the team shorts.

I wonder if it's the referee's job to enforce this rule as well? Former Socceroo and Brisbane Strikers player, Frank Farina, admitted he's never been asked to prove the colour of his underpants and says that because it's usually too difficult to find undies that match team shorts, it's easier to go without them.

While the ref has the leading role with the whistle, he is always backed up by two support staff, known as linesmen. These guys decide when a ball is in or out of the field of play, which team is awarded a corner kick, kick at goal or throw-in and let the ref know when a team wishes to make a substitution. Like AFL goal umpires, soccer linesmen perform their duties with little coloured flags – usually bright red, yellow or lime green, anything suitably out of fashion, basically.

One of the other entertaining aspects of an international soccer game is watching the referees and players argue over a decision. Neutral referees are put in control of international matches which often results in two countries and one referee all speaking different languages. While nobody understands anybody else, you'll be able to guess most of the conversation by the gestures made all round.

Corner kick

Corner kicks are awarded to the attacking team if the ball rolls over the goal line and was last touched by a defending player.

If the ball rolls over the goal line and was last touched by an attacking player, play will re-start with a goal kick from the defender's goal keeper.

If the ball rolls over the touchline, play will restart with a throw-in by the non-offending team.

Four most common signals from referees

PENALTY KICK: Referee blows his whistle and with one arm points to the penalty mark.

GOAL: Point to the goal area indicates a goal has been kicked.

DIRECT FREE KICK: With a whistle blow the referee will indicate the direction the kick will take.

INDIRECT FREE KICK: One arm raised above the head will be maintained until the kick has been taken and play continues.

Two most common signals from linesmen

CORNER KICK: A raised arm, positioned horizontally, points to the corner where the kick will be taken.

OFFSIDE: A raised flag indicates a player is offside.

Penalty kick   **Goal**   **Direct free kick**   **Indirect free kick**

FULL TIME

Con the coach either has steam coming out of his orifices or he has a wry smile on his face like that of a puppeteer who's pulled all the right strings. If the team has won, Con shouts the drinks all night out of his own pocket (until he can claim expenses on Monday morning), but if the team has lost, he sends all the guys straight back onto the park after the game for a three-hour training session while he goes back to the club and lets all the distressed wives shout him a drink or two.

Soccer coaches are pretty much in a win–win situation – until the end of the season, of course, when they jump back on the merry-go-round looking for their next home.

Hopefully, you'll be enthused to go to as many soccer games as you can fit into your schedule. Club competition is good, but internationals are awesome. The atmosphere at a big soccer game is probably one of the best you'll find anywhere. The spectators are knowledgeable, usually, and get right behind specific players and their teams. Chanting is often heard from soccer crowds and, of course, being a part of the Mexican wave when the whole stadium is committed to it is wonderful. You'll be walking on air as you leave the ground.

Offside

4 RUG

A QUICK HISTORY LESSON

Although modern man has had arms for centuries, it wasn't until the 1800s that one exceedingly clever fellow named William Webb Ellis discovered we could use them!

Playing soccer at an English school in Rugby, Warwickshire, little William got so bored with kicking the ball about that he decided to pick it up and run with it. Eye witnesses originally thought he was trying to steal the ball – nobody had ever seen anything like it! He was reprimanded for being such a goose but the telling of the story spread throughout England and inquisitive types decided they would have a go at the game played in Rugby.

The idea caught on and the game began to be played in schools. The 'Rugby Union' was formed in 1872 and the game spread internationally. Originally, points could only be scored by kicking goals, but gradually the idea of scoring through a 'try' was accepted.

There was even a brief moment of Olympic fame for the game, with rugby contested at the 1900, 1908, 1920 and 1924 games. Australia's first-ever touring rugby team was playing in the British Isles at the time of the Olympics and decided to enter. We won gold by beating England 32-3.

Unfortunately, rugby didn't stay on the Olympic schedule because it was played in too few countries.

It's about male bonding. It's about tweed jackets and polite little claps – not raucous, meat pie behaviour. The game has developed two styles – the kicking game, favoured by the Northern Hemisphere nations, and the running game, preferred by Australia and New Zealand. In other words, skill with the boot is more important north of the equator, while down south we like the ducking, weaving, athletic style of play.

The perception has been that rugby union is about accountants, stockbrokers and lawyers having a bit of weekend fun. This professional influence on the game means that there are no rules in rugby – rather the game is played according to certain laws. The players are all so conscious of how they are going to look on the trading floor on Monday that they wouldn't dare contemplate behaviour which may result in broken noses, black eyes or missing teeth. So who needs rules? These tertiary trained gentlemen know how to behave. Rugby union is about biffo without the biff.

Rugby is like golf in many ways. Plenty of business is done while playing the game. For instance, in what is called the 'lineout', the opposing teams line up alongside each other while one of the players yells out a series of numbers before throwing the ball down the line for somebody to snatch. The numbers he's chanting are in fact how many shares he's got left from Friday trading – he's simply offering everybody a cheap investment deal on some blue chip stock. The gesture is received warmly by both

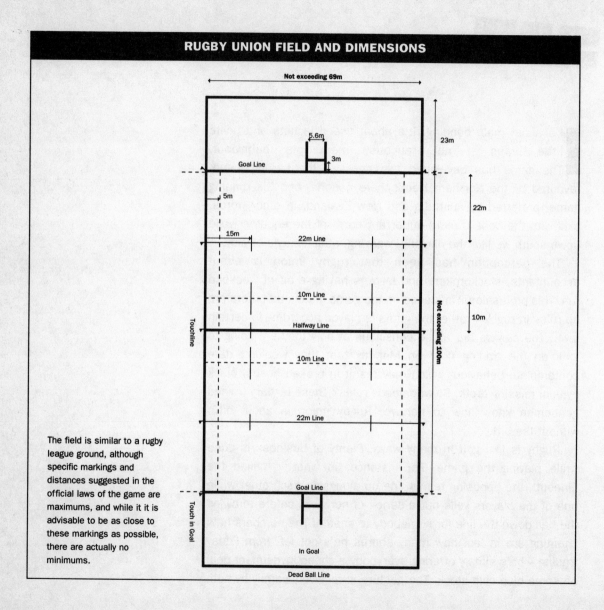

RUGBY UNION FIELD AND DIMENSIONS

Not exceeding 69m

5.6m

3m

23m

Goal Line

5m

22m

15m

22m Line

10m Line

10m

Touchline

Halfway Line

Not exceeding 100m

10m Line

22m Line

Touch in Goal

Goal Line

In Goal

Dead Ball Line

The field is similar to a rugby league ground, although specific markings and distances suggested in the official laws of the game are maximums, and while it it is advisable to be as close to these markings as possible, there are actually no minimums.

sides, and whichever team takes up the offer usually scores from it. You will notice sections of the crowd clapping when a lineout has been won. That's because they are the directors of the company which has just raised its share value through on-field activities.

THE PLAYERS

Like rugby league, the players in each team have a job to do according to the number of their jumper.

There are props, flankers and hookers. There are locks, halfbacks, fullbacks, flyhalves, wingers and centres. There are also No.8s. It is rumoured that No.8s don't like to be limited to any one position and hence haven't been given a positional title. They like to roam freely both on and off the field.

Australia's Tim Gavin is the No.8 of all No.8s. He is a true legend in the game. He roams around the NSW countryside when he's not playing in a Wallaby jersey, he roams around Sydney city when he's not playing for his Randwick club, and he roams around Italy with former Prime Minister Silvio Berlusconi when he's not playing up. I don't know why they don't just call No.8s roamers – or even aromas, given that they can sniff action from a mile away.

Let's run through the fifteen positions on a rugby union team:

1&3. PROPS: Just as the name suggests, these guys prop up the front row of the scrum on the field, and they carry the kitbag of toys that are played with off the field. Rugby union toys are mostly professional games such as Monopoly and Scruples.

2. HOOKER: The hooker unites the front row of the scrum by hugging a prop on either side. Hookers keep the side together and are often referred to as family types for their great love of being close to their team mates.

4 & 5. LOCKS: Just as we use locks to keep our cars and houses safe, rugby locks are inserted into the front row of a scrum in order to protect the rest of the side. The locks keep the door shut against the opposition and maintain ground that the side has made by pushing the scrum forwards into opposition territory. Locks also have a role in lineouts – their talents are many! Most locks consider themselves on a par with Air Jordan, and leap into the atmosphere during a lineout to grab the throw-in ball.

6 & 7. FLANKERS: These are the goodtime boys; they are everywhere. Looking for trouble on the field? Hunt out the flankers. They huddle around scrums, hang at the back of lineouts and are generally close to the ball no matter where it is. They are fast movers, fast talkers and players to be wary of.

No. 8: As we mentioned earlier, the No. 8s are special people. They are the meat in the sandwich…they are the glue between fronts and backs and need to work hard to keep the team together. As far as what they really do on the field – it's anyone's guess. They are always personable people, though, so I suggest you go watch a game of rugby union, go back to the club afterwards and share a drink with the team No. 8. He'll tell you all sorts of wonderful things about what No. 8s can do. He might even be able to explain what he does on the field.

9. HALFBACK: You don't need to be a halfwit to be a halfback; quite the contrary. Halfbacks are probably the fullwits of the team. They think on behalf of the rest of their team mates. Halfbacks ALWAYS have the ball. If you see someone running with the ball, he's probably the halfback. He feeds the scrum, then races around behind the scrum to get the ball back, then he feeds it out to his line of backs before joining the end of the queue to receive it again. To be a halfback you need to be a genius. You need to

RUGBY UNION FIELD POSITIONS

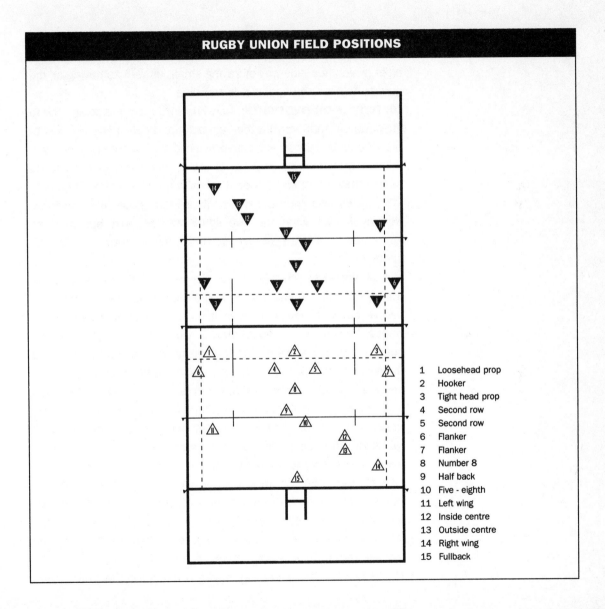

1. Loosehead prop
2. Hooker
3. Tight head prop
4. Second row
5. Second row
6. Flanker
7. Flanker
8. Number 8
9. Half back
10. Five - eighth
11. Left wing
12. Inside centre
13. Outside centre
14. Right wing
15. Fullback

'read' the game and predict what will happen next and organise the team into the appropriate positions. You need to be quick and agile (which is a nice way of saying small) as well as having all the guts to tackle the opposition's frontline.

10. FLYHALF OR FIVE-EIGHTH: Also known as the magician. These guys work in tandem with the halfbacks and determine the flow of play. Recently retired Australian five-eighth, Michael Lynagh, was brilliant to watch. He knew what the opposition was going to do before they did it, so he'd beat them to it. Five-eighths run, duck, kick, tackle and keep the rest of their team mates on their toes. Nobody knows what the five-eighth will do next but you can guarantee it will be spectacular. Their off-field antics are just as spectacular, apparently.

11 & 14. WINGERS: Also known as Campo. David Campese is the winger the world wants, but Australia has. He is the one man that people call a goose and mean it as a compliment. Campo has what's known as a goose step – while he's flying down the outside, heading towards the tryline, he will interrupt his running rhythm with a little pause before resuming his natural flow. The delay is enough to throw his opponents off track and leave him a clear path to run through and score. Every other winger in the world wants to be Campo. Wingers hang around the touchline waiting for the ball. Once it's in their grasp they make a charge for the goal line in order to score a try.

12 & 13. CENTRES: Centres are the workers of the backline who rarely get any credit. Centres need to feel the pace of the game, determine its direction and feed the wingers at exactly the right moment to allow them to score. Centres are like co-stars. They do most of the hard work and get very little praise.

15. FULLBACK: Also known as fall back, because if anything goes wrong, the entire team can blame the fullback. Why not? He's the last line of attack and defence so it must be his fault if something stuffs up. The fullback is the lonely guy standing between the goalposts with nobody to talk to. He's crucial in catching and kicking and taking the blame. Never marry a fullback. You'd have very few friends.

COACHES

Rugby union coaches are paid to confuse. If the players don't know what the coach is on about, chances are the opposition won't have a clue either – somehow that's supposed to give your team an advantage. Another plus is that the media and the public won't have any idea about the coach's plan and therefore can't be critical. If you don't know what the coach is trying to say it's very difficult to criticise.

Most rugby union coaches have either a degree in philosophy or are very good con-artists.

Rugby coaches are deep. They are meaningful. They command admiration internationally and, after retiring, they normally take up Honorary Doctorates at well recognised universities and go on to teach thousands of others about the beauty of confusion.

If ever you start to think life is easy, or simple, I suggest you go and have a chat to your local rugby coach. He'll sort you out in minutes and more often than not won't even charge you.

START THE CLOCK

Rugby Union is entering a new era. The game is going from pseudo-amateur status (where the players were considered amateur despite earning lots of money for off-field performances like turning up to lunches, dinners, etc.) to professionalism.

RUGBY UNION FAN: JULIE KEARNS

Women worldwide envy Julie Kearns and most of them don't even know her. Julie married Wallaby captain Phil Kearns, ending the hopes and desires of the millions of females who have watched every moving piece of Phil as he skippered Australia.

Julie's shocking admission is that she didn't even need a game plan to earn Phil's attention and devotion...

'My knowledge of a game plan and all that stuff isn't that great but I know enough to follow a match. A few of my friends from university played so I went along to watch, and that's what sparked my interest.

'Studying for a degree in physical education, I had an avid interest in all sport, but footy wasn't on top of my priorities. It was a bit of a blur to start with, but if you get thrown in at the deep end you learn quickly. It's a bit daunting at first, but once you identify with one or two people you start to relate pretty easily.'

Rugby has long been used by businessmen as a social arena in which they make new contacts, and women are starting to get in on the act too.

'The social scene is great, We never have a moment to ourselves – there are always functions and various things organised and the girls and guys work really well together. It varies though – in Sydney the girls only get together when the boys are playing footy but in Queensland the Union make it their business to get the girls involved in all sorts of things, so they are really close and spend a lot of time together. It's a great network.'

Social scene aside, learning to appreciate the game and its technical aspects isn't all that hard.

'You can enjoy rugby on a couple of different levels...you can sit next to somebody who knows the rules and get them to educate you so that your husband takes your advice seriously when you decide to give it, or you can just go along to check out the good-looking guys on the field and work out who's worth chatting to at the bar later on that night.'

Of course, Julie only ever chats up Phil these days.

With the number of international games on each year now, players can't afford to keep fulltime jobs and give their all to the sport, so contracts are being worked out, players are being signed up by the Rugby Union and will start being paid what they are worth. The irony is, a lot of them are worth more off the field as professional executives, than on it as professional players. Some of them might have been better off under the old system.

While the obligatory coin toss is conducted to determine which team will run in which direction and the referee blows his whistle to start the clock, the game doesn't actually begin until the fullbacks determine who is the best kicker. This relates to the kicking game mentioned earlier, favoured by Northern Hemisphere countries. Say Australia kicks off and Micky Magic boots the ball down into Irish territory. Ireland's fullback, Mickey Mouse, will endeavour to catch the ball and boot it straight back into Aussie territory. Billy Brave then gets his chance. He catches the ball and boots it back even harder to Mickey Mouse, who struggles to take the catch and put in another kick. This goes on for four or five minutes, until one of the captains gets sick and tired of this display of manhood and tells his fullback to run with the ball next time he gets it. This is when the crowd wakes up and starts to cheer their team with emotive lines like 'great run, old boy' and 'straight up the middle, son'.

Wouldn't phrases like that motivate you? They work on rugby union players, believe me. Keep your wits about you – the next 40 minutes is going to provide an abundance of activity before the coaches bring down the sponges and oranges at halftime.

You'll witness scrummages, rucks, mauls, tackles, kicks, lineouts and tries like you've never seen before. Thirty men from two sides will all be pretending they are Alexander the Great, Julius Caesar or King Arthur fighting for their people. And they are. They are fighting for you – the crowd. Fighting to score points and notch up another win so you can feel proud that you are being protected by such powerful, intellectual, battle-brave men.

Rugby union is for thinkers. As part of the crowd you must think too. Never get carried away and scream ridiculous comments like you would at other football grounds. Whenever a play is made you must analyse it and make some deep, emotional comment, such as 'I'm not so sure he should have done that'. Aim to sound like the coach – that way other spectators won't fully understand what you're referring to and won't be able to criticise your interpretation of the game.

Minutes after the ref has started his clock and team A decides to run with the ball, you will notice team B closing in on the player with the ball. Prepare for a maul.

MAULS

If the player with the ball is tackled but remains on his feet, a pack called a maul will form. The player with the ball will try and get it out to one of his team mates while the opposition tries to wrestle the ball free.

Maul

Ruck

RUCKS

If the player with the ball is brought to the ground, he must release it immediately, while the players form a type of scrum around him to try and heel the ball back into their possession – this is called a ruck.

Once the ball finds space to breathe, it is passed along the backline again to the centres, wingers and fullback, who aim to score a try. Often rucks and mauls collapse, which means the ref will call for a scrum. The team in possession before the collapse will feed the ball into the scrum.

SCRUM

The forwards form a pack in one of two formations preferred by the team and coach: a 3-2-3, fairly uncommon these days, or a 3-4-1. The numbers refer to the number of players in each row of the scrum. A 3-2-3 formation consists of the hooker between two props in the front row, the two locks make up the second row, and the flankers and No.8 in the back row. Alternatively, a team may prefer to have the two locks and two flankers make up the second row with only the No.8 as a third row, ie. the 3-4-1 formation.

For any minor infringement the referee may call for a scrum to restart play. Part of the intrigue of a rugby union scrum is the way

Scrum

it can twist and turn as the forwards from both teams act out a power play. Jostling for ground in this way is legal as teams try to earn as much ground as possible from their opponents or try to confuse the opposition with constant movement so that they aren't too sure where the ball will emerge.

If, however, the scrum twists more than 90 degrees, the ref will order it to be re-fed. (*Feeding the scrum* is the term used for throwing the ball in between the two packs to restart play.) Having fed the scrum, the halfback races around behind his pack and waits for the ball to emerge before distributing it to his flyhalf and the backline, which will head for the tryline.

LINEOUT

If the ball goes over the touchline, a lineout will be held. The forwards from both teams line up alongside each other at right angles to the touchline. Player No.2 (the hooker) from the non-offending side will throw the ball in, straight down the centre while the forwards from either side spring into the air like basketballers aiming for a slam dunk, with the sole purpose of getting the ball to one of their team mates for another chance of scoring.

Lineout
In this diagram team ▲ has the ball to throw into the lineout.

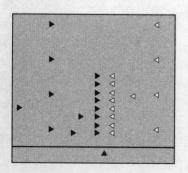

Lineout

TRY

Scoring a try in rugby union is similar to scoring one in rugby league. Comparing them though is like comparing the Aussie dollar to the US dollar.

Because of the number of stockbrokers working in rugby union the try has been inflated. In rugby league it's worth four points. In rugby union it's worth five. A player must race, dive or jump across the goal line, between the touchlines, and place the ball firmly on the ground. Now what's the difference? Why should it be worth a point more in rugby union than in rugby league? I suppose it's like buying Christian Dior pantyhose compared to Home Brand. They do the same job but one is, supposedly, classier.

87

CONVERSION

Once a try is scored and the team mates all hug and kiss and pat each other's bottoms, a conversion attempt will be made. In other words, the kicker of the team will try to boot the ball between the goalposts and over the crossbar to earn an extra 2 points. So a converted try in rugby union is worth a total of 7 points. (In the deflated 'league' market a converted try is worth only 6 points.)

While the conversion is attempted, both teams ready themselves for the next phase of play, but don't you be distracted and take your eyes off the kicker – you are about to see some of the most entertaining dance steps you'll find anywhere. Some goal kickers do a little quickstep before pouncing on the ball, others have gone for the South American influence and try the samba before moving in. Others do an African war dance while some attempt a ballerina plié.

Goal kicking used to be a simple matter of taking a two or three step run-up and striking the ball. Today, with the focus being on entertainment, kickers have a private competition to see who can come up with the most complicated approach. The result is that if a kicker runs 'around the corner' to kick the ball and throws in a couple of knee bends on the approach, he looks like a genius for achieving something so difficult. On the other hand, if he misses, he looks like a real turkey.

OFFSIDE

When attacking, players must remain behind the ball. When defending, players must maintain a distance of ten metres between themselves and the line of attack. During a lineout, the backline players must stay ten metres back from the line of touch (an imaginary line running between the forwards of each team).

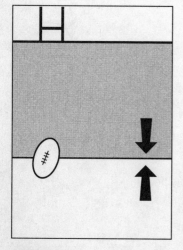

Offside rule
Players from each team must remain behind an imaginary line through the ball.

OTHER WAYS TO SCORE

Other than scoring a try and converting it, there are three other ways of scoring in rugby union.

1. *If a penalty is awarded by the referee and you are in goal-kicking territory, you can attempt a penalty goal. If successful, three points will be added to the team's tally.*

2. *A drop goal is a goal kicked in the general run of play – all of a sudden Billy Plonk finds himself unable to score a try (worth five points) but in a perfect position to kick a drop goal. If successful he will earn three points for the team.*

3. *A penalty try can be awarded by the ref if he thinks a try would have been scored had the opposition not interfered illegally. A penalty try is worth five points.*

So, after 40 minutes of nonstop entertainment, the ref blows his whistle to signal halftime.

The teams gather in two little groups on the sideline, the coach comes down for his halftime address (which nobody understands) and the players all suck on oranges. The big question these days is, 'What's in the oranges?' Looking at some of the forwards, you might be tempted to think that their oranges had been spiked with steroids. Some players are so big and muscly that they no longer have necks, waists or ankles. They are rump steak all over. The truth is these players are just typical examples of the average Aussie male. One hooker told me his strength came from lifting his brief case each night after collecting his percentage from stock market deals. I believe him.

SECOND HALF

Ditto the first half.

COMMON PENALTIES

- *Accepting the ball while offside*
- *Tackling a player from an offside position*
- *Not letting go of the ball after being tackled*
- *Forward pass*
- *Dangerous or high tackle*
- *Foul play*
- *Misconduct*

REFEREES AND TOUCH JUDGES

Referees have their hands full – not just with big burly players, and the ever present judgemental crowd – but in rugby union they must keep the score as well as the regular duties of keeping time and administering the laws of the game.

Fitness is of prime importance, although some players would argue that referees should spend more time learning the rules of the game instead of concentrating on their strength and stamina. This is just sour grapes. Rugby union referees, like all sports referees, can't get to the top without first memorising all of the laws of the game. The problem arises from the interpretation of the laws which inevitably differs between players and refs.

One referee controls each game and he or she is assisted by two touch judges – one patrolling each side of the ground.

High tackle

Free kick

Penalty kick

Try

Scrum

Six most common signals from referees:

HIGH OR DANGEROUS TACKLE: One arm outstretched while the other moves across the front of the neck.

FREE KICK: One raised arm, bent at the elbow, indicates a free kick while the other arm is used to point to the team awarded the free kick.

PENALTY KICK: One arm raised at a 60° angle while the other arm indicates the team awarded the penalty.

TRY: The referee stands where the try was scored, blows his whistle and stretches one arm above his head.

SCRUM: Points to position where scrum should be taken and outstretches other arm to indicate which team will feed the ball.

NOT RELEASING THE BALL: Arms folded across the chest.

FULLTIME

Being part of a rugby union crowd carries extra responsibilities. Firstly, you can't get up and leave early to avoid the car park rush. In rugby union, no matter how one-sided the game is, you stay till the end. It's a great way of ensuring that everybody sees who's keeping company with who and what sort of car they're driving. Check out the wives' new Gucci shoes and the husbands' latest imported diving watches before zapping the alarm on your prestige sports car.

]Many people haven't enjoyed the experience of watching a game of rugby union because they've been too embarrassed about arriving in their resprayed Holden Kingswood. Don't let this stop you! Haven't you realised why rugby union games are played early on Saturday afternoons instead of late on Sundays? It's so you can test drive the latest Merc from your nearest dealer...

Not releasing the ball

RUGBY UNION FAN: KATRINA HORAN

Before marrying the Queensland and Australian rugby union centre, Tim Horan, Katrina followed the game and learned a fair bit about it growing up with a rugby-mad dad.

'We lived a fair way out of Toowoomba so we never saw any games live but we watched every international ever shown on TV – my dad especially loved the Tests against the All Blacks.

'Early on my three sisters and I didn't know what was going on in the game because we were too busy playing netball and tennis, but by 17 everything fell into place.'

Meanwhile Katrina met Tim at school during year 11 and by midway through year 12 they were going out .

'In the beginning I used to go along to Tim's games for the social scene – everybody always goes out together after a game and after Test matches there's a Test dinner. The social part of rugby is great . . . you meet friends all the way through.

'As I got older though, I've realised the importance of winning and the value of the game financially, so I probably take it a bit more seriously now.'

During 1995 Tim made an incredible comeback to state and international rugby after going through a traumatic knee reconstruction which placed a lot of pressure on both Tim and Katrina.

'We were told many times that Tim wouldn't be the player he used to be and that his career was under threat.

I realised how dangerous the game could be. But being the person he is – so positive – we got through it all.

'He was so determined and put in so much hard work so I felt confident that he'd be right back up there. It was tough early on though because he couldn't move for months – I had to shower him, dress him, everything. When he started on the comeback trail he had to fly to Sydney every two weeks for a fortnight of physio therapy and work on his leg . . . he'd be home for two weeks, gone for two. So when he was re-called for Queensland I thought it was really well deserved. I always thought he was a better player than the others anyway, I'm probably biased though', Katrina giggled.

'It's hard to explain the stress in seeing somebody who his at the top of their career all of a sudden go to the bottom and have to fight all the way back, so when he went to South Africa for the 1995 World Cup and was called back into the starting lineup for Australia I was so proud – he's such a special player, he always plays with a spark.

'When Australia was knocked out, though, it was devastating. All the wives and girlfriends used to get together at one of our houses to watch the games and when Australia went down to England in the last couple of minutes we were all distraught. Then reality hit and we thought oh no, the guys will be coming home early, we'd better all tidy up our houses!'

you drive it straight to the game, watch the match, brag throughout the game to those sitting around you, and then watch them drool as you drive off (straight back to the dealer). It works every time.

If anyone starts to catch on and asks with a degree of suspicion why you drive a different car each weekend just tell them it's one of the perks of your job. If they catch on, and ask what you do for a living, I suggest you start supporting another team.

Another responsibility you have as being part of the 'ruggers' crowd is that you MUST join your friends back at the club for some chicken and champagne. Accept politely. You'll realise, as soon as you get to the club and the boys in the team have showered and dressed, that the celebration technique is just like in any other

footy code. A couple of beers, a couple of far-fetched stories about heroics during the game, and some Chinese takeaway to polish off the day.

Rugby union is a very sociable game. The players and supporters are a friendly bunch who will welcome you warmly. One unique aspect of rugby union is the fact that there are no barriers separating the players from anybody else. It's one big happy family which you will enjoy being a part of.

5 RUGBY

LEAGUE

A QUICK HISTORY LESSON

Rugby league is an offshoot of rugby union, which itself was an offshoot of soccer. Lost you already? It's simple – first there was a river, then came a wash basin, now there are washing machines. Sport has basically developed along the same lines as our laundering habits. Some of you may not even do your own washing any more: you probably take it to the laundromat to be done for you. Perhaps in footballing terms this is what 'Superleague' is all about...it surpasses all other options. It promises bigger, better games, it's the elite of the elite, it's not just A-grade, it's A-plus.

Back in 1895 at the George Hotel in Huddersfield, Yorkshire, a number of rugby teams from the north of England met to discuss the pay-for-play concept (that's what they told their wives anyway!). Most of the men involved in the game had to give up their Saturday afternoon work shifts (in the mines, on the railroads, etc.) and they were losing more money than they could afford to from their pay packets. At the time, it meant that the working class man found it virtually impossible to continue playing.

But amateur sport was all the rage. The idea of being paid to play sport was considered cheap and nasty, and athletes were banned if it was found they had earned money for competing. A vote was taken 'that professionalism should not be allowed' and the result was 282 votes for and 136 votes against. However in economic terms, pure amateurism was no longer viable for the footballers, so, against all the rules, and despite the vote that had been taken, professional football was born – in a pub on a bleak English day. And the pub culture has remained part of rugby league ever since. The Northern Union, as it was then called, set up its own headquarters and changed some of the rules to give the new game its own look.

In Australia, a similar breakaway occurred in 1907-1908 when an argument erupted over the payment of medical bills for injured players. In 1922 the name of the game became rugby league and it was played with pride by the working class.

WHAT THE GAME IS ALL ABOUT

The aim is for one team to score more points than the other. This happens both on the field and off it. ON the field you compete *with* your team mates, OFF the field you compete *against* your team mates. On the field you score points by playing footy, off the field you score points in any number of ways – telling the most outrageous story in the pub, consuming most beers, chatting up most women, being a hit on the dance floor, that sort of thing. Surprisingly, a player's reputation off the field is carried with him onto the field. Opponents fear him because of what he can do AFTER a game as much as for what he can do during it.

This tradition developed in order to help the player with potential. In case he never reaches legendary status on the field, he has this second opportunity to achieve such status.

Unlike other codes of football, every team has two home grounds rather than one. The first is the oval where the game is played, the second is the leagues club where the celebrating is done afterwards and where 'potentially' good players are often found even during a game. 'Down the Leagues' is a phrase all footyheads will hear and often use. Players are either playing, training or down the Leagues, ie. at the club, building their reputation in other areas. You can understand why the pressure of being a league star is enormous – people expect great things from you at all times, not just for the 80 minutes each weekend when you're on the field.

RUGBY LEAGUE FIELD AND DIMENSIONS

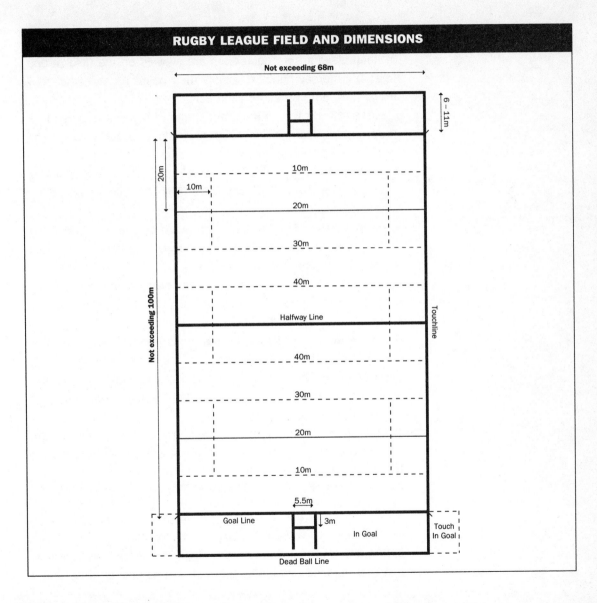

PLAYERS

Thirteen players from each team are allowed on the field at one time. Their jersey numbers signify their positions and what they are best at, both on and off the field.

1. FULLBACK: On the field – the last line of defence and used for powerful, precision kicking. Off the field – displays the same qualities – the precise and defensive type.

2. RIGHT WINGER: On the field – patrols the right touchline and is a speedy player used to score tries. Off the field – fast talker, scores quickly.

3. RIGHT CENTRE: On the field – works inside the right winger, is fast and determines the direction of play. Off the field – works fast but scores less often than a winger.

4. LEFT CENTRE: On the field – does the same as the right centre but on the left side of the ground. Off the field – ignores the barriers and works both sides of any crowd.

5. LEFT WINGER: On the field – patrols left touchline, is fast and scores often. Off the field – aims to score several times in one night.

6. FIVE EIGHTH: On the field – a tricky player who controls the flow of a game and is a precision kicker. Off the field – an intelligent type who remains in control.

7. HALF BACK: On the field – fast and accurate, works the scrum, and dictates the direction of play along with the five-eighth. Off the field – fast and accurate, works any room well.

8 & 10. FRONT ROW FORWARDS (PROPS): On the field – big and mean, used to make ground in powerful surges and to crunch the opposition attackers. Off the field – displays bursts of passion which can knock you down if you are unprepared.

9. HOOKER: On the field – at the centre of the three-man front row, used for hooking or winning the ball in a scrum, at least that's

FIELD POSITIONS

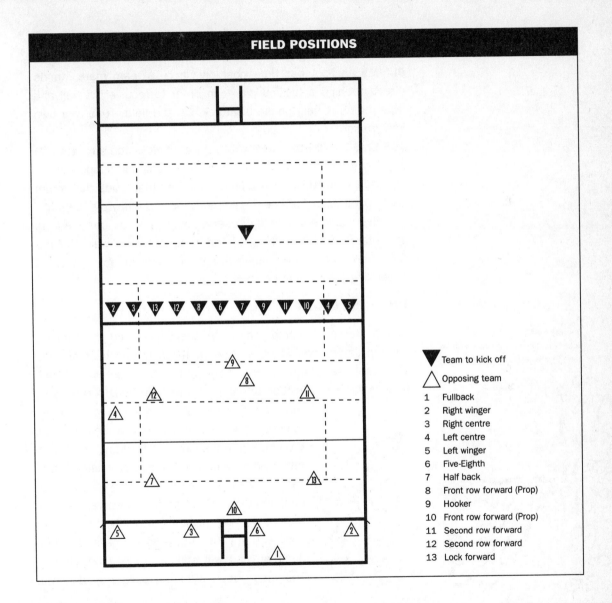

▼ Team to kick off

△ Opposing team

1 Fullback
2 Right winger
3 Right centre
4 Left centre
5 Left winger
6 Five-Eighth
7 Half back
8 Front row forward (Prop)
9 Hooker
10 Front row forward (Prop)
11 Second row forward
12 Second row forward
13 Lock forward

how it used to be before the scrum became a joke and the ball was allowed to go through to the second row. Also acts as **DUMMY HALF**: A part-time position where a team mate stands directly behind a tackled player in order to receive the ball and determine the next phase of attack. Off the field – use your own imagination.

11 & 12. SECOND ROW FORWARDS: On the field – add strength and support to the front row. Off the field – strong and supportive.

13. LOCK FORWARD: On the field – the key that holds the scrum pack together. Off the field – holds the key to many a situation.

Other numbers identify reserve players who are used as substitutes to replace tired, injured or out-of-form players. Off the field these guys are usually fresh and looking for a way of expending their unused energy.

START THE CLOCK

Dummy half
Positioned behind the player who has been tackled and is 'playing' the ball.

At the start of a game the ref tosses a coin and the winning captain determines which way he wants to run in the first half. This may seem like a menial task, but in fact captains almost need a tertiary education to carry out this role. Considerations in

making this choice involve wind direction, wind speed, crowd noise, favourite end of the ground, where the girlfriend is sitting and, most importantly, where the television cameras are set up. Captains want their team to establish a good lead in the first half, so they want all the factors working in their favour. By the second half, with any luck the wind will have changed direction and will still be working with them. The wind speed will have picked up and will

RUGBY LEAGUE FAN: GIL WISHART

Gil Wishart was one of us. She was rambling through life, having a pretty good time of it, knowing that there was this thing called football but not paying too much attention to it. Then a guy called Rod appeared. He had all the right lines. He even offered to shout Gil a drink one night and it was at that moment that her life changed. She became involved with a SNAF.

Rod Wishart is one of those lovable country lads blessed with the speed of lightning and the kick of a wild mule. These have earnt him goalkicking duties and a spot on the wing for both NSW and for Australia.

'I didn't know a thing about rugby league before I met Rod. At first I didn't know what all the hype was about when we'd walk down the street and everybody knew who he was and wanted to talk with him. I had no idea I'd been living in the dark for so long and didn't realise how big this footy syndrome was!

'I was actually disappointed when I found out Rod was a footballer because of the reputation they all have...you know, they have a stigma attached to them because supposedly they all drink too much and party too hard. They're meant to be loud and unfaithful...but I've since found out it's just not true.'

Being a relatively new convert to footy, Gil's aware that she still has plenty to learn but says the game's thrilling without any specialist knowledge.

'There's still plenty I don't understand, like penalties and things, but I've got a good grasp on the basics...I know which way the ball's going, and I know if Rod's got the ball. I know when a try is scored, sometimes...and that's all you need, really.

'The social side is really good. Football people are a really good bunch. All the girls get on really well and there are other advantages of being involved with someone that plays the game – Rod supposedly gets to spend lots of days at home. If he didn't surf and play golf he might be at home!

'A lot of people think it must be difficult being a footballer's wife but I love sport and play a bit myself so I know about the ups and downs and can understand the emotional side. Actually, Rod comes to watch me play netball sometimes but he just gets bombarded by fans.

'There are disadvantages, such as when they're away for long periods of time, but I think it's worse for him because he's the one without everybody. I'm still at home with the baby and family and friends; he's the one alone. Also, when he gets injured I think, 'Oh, why don't you just give it away?' But that's always towards the end of the season and it's just like school – you get sick of it all but after the holidays you realise it isn't that bad and you're actually ready to go back.

'Plus I know it's all short-lived: you can't play footy forever, so you've got to make the most of it while you can.'

help in attack. Crowd noise will be feverishly in support of the team. The girlfriends will have moved to the other end of the ground so they can see how brilliant their loved-ones are when they're charging down the field, and the television cameras...well, if they're playing that sensationally they won't be off them, will they? As you can see, it's a lot for a captain to think of in one quick coin toss, isn't it?

Once this difficult choice has been made, and the crowd has been kept in suspense for at least three seconds, the opposing team kicks off from the centre of the halfway line into your team's half of the ground. This is where your forwards get into some heavy work running the ball up, making ground, and hopefully breaking down the opposing team's line of defence. Any player who has the ball can be legally tackled.

THE TACKLE

A player can only be tackled if in possession of the ball. If a player without the ball is tackled, a penalty will be awarded to the innocent party. Tackles can be made by any number of opponents and can be made on any part of the body from the feet to the shoulders – anything above that is head high and can result in the guilty party being sent off for the rest of the game with an appointment at the judiciary for further suspension. The judiciary is likely to enforce a 2-6 week holiday for such action.

A team has only six tackles to make its way up to the opponent's goal line and score a try. The referee will signal once five tackles have been made. At this point there are two choices: keep running the ball in the hope of making the goal line (if unsuccessful the ball must simply be handed over to the opposition) or, if there is no chance of scoring a try, the ball is kicked as deeply as possible into

Tackle

opposition territory so they then have further to run to score their own try. If all six tackles are made, the ball will be turned over, or handed over to the opposition.

If at any stage during the six tackles, the ball is touched by an opponent, the tackle count restarts. Once a player has been tackled, he must stand upright, facing his opponents' goal line, and drop or place the ball on the ground before passing it behind with his foot to a waiting team mate, called a dummy half.

THE BALL

The ball can only be passed backwards or in a straight line relative to the direction a team is running – never forwards. If it is knocked forward accidentally by a team mate and makes contact with the ground, it is deemed a knock-on, and a scrum is called. If it is passed forward deliberately or otherwise it is called a forward pass and a penalty kick is given against the offending team.

Scrum
This illustration shows one half (one team) packed down only.

THE SCRUM

Once a scrum has been called, for a misdemeanour, the halfback of the innocent team is supposed to throw the ball into the centre of the scrum, giving each team a fair chance of playing footsies with each other before winning the ball, kicking it out the back to their runners and, they hope, scoring a try. These days, though, halfbacks seem to be able to throw the ball into their own second row of the scrum, meaning certain possession for their side, leaving the front rowers to entertain themselves in other ways. Eye gouging, ear biting and whispering sweet nothings are some of the games front rowers favour these days – all done in fun, of course, with no permanent damage being sustained.

KNOCK ON

Having 'good hands' is crucial in rugby league because so much of the game is played with the hands. Accurate passing is a prime component of the game, as is control. Every now and then the ball slips from a player's grasp and is fumbled forward onto the ground – this is called a knock on. Wet conditions can increase the frequency of handling errors, as can extremely hot and humid conditions which make the ball greasy. A scrum is formed when a team knocks on.

TRIES

Tries are scored by a player who places the ball on the ground anywhere on or behind the opponents' goal line, with no part of his body outside the touchline. A try is worth four points and earns the scoring team the opportunity of kicking a goal to convert the try.

Referees and touch judges are crucial in awarding tries – many times a player is 'held up' by the opposition, which means they may have gone over the goal line but haven't been able to place the ball on the ground because of clever tackling. If the player is held up, play will restart with a scrum.

An eight point try can occur when a player has been illegally tackled in the process of scoring a try. The try is awarded and the goal kicker is allowed two attempts at goal – one from the point where the try is scored, and the second from directly in front of the uprights.

Try

CONVERSION

Once a try has been scored, the team's appointed goal-kicker (usually the fullback) lines the ball up for a conversion. A successful conversion kick is one which passes between the two upright posts and over the cross bar, and is worth two points. The kick used is called a place kick: the ball is placed on the field, usually a bucket of sand is provided to create a little mound for the ball to sit on, and the kicker approaches the ball with a run-up.

In case you're wondering why the kicker always tries to convert from a most ridiculous angle, there is an explanation. The kick must be taken from a point in line with where the try was scored If the try was scored right in the corner of the field then the ball must be placed in line with the corner. This is why you'll see most try scorers trying to get in as close as possible to the goalposts – to make a conversion attempt easier. The distance out from the goal posts depends solely on how far back the kicker needs to go to get the best angle for the conversion.

FIELD GOALS

Although worth only one point, field goals have won many games If a team is in front of the goal posts, and it doesn't look like they'll be able to get through the defence to score a try, one option is to pop up a shot at goal, and, if successful, score a handy point. Field goals are also used as buffers: if one side is already a converted try ahead, that is, six points in front, the addition of a field goal gives that little extra edge. The opponents will then need more than one converted try of their own to catch up.

Surprisingly, games have also been lost by field goals. Occasionally, good kickers fancy themselves, and can't help booting one through every time they get near the posts, even when they might have had a winger or a centre in a perfect position to score a try. The players who make this mistake are known as mirrorballs – they're the sort of people who are so busy worrying about themselves and how they look, that they forget about the overall game plan. These are the same players found loitering in car parks looking at their own window reflections after the match, or the ones that get caught watching themselves in the mirror at discos.

PENALTIES

If a team deliberately breaks the rules of the game, such as elbowing, headbutting, obstruction, stiff arming an opponent, etc., the ref will award a penalty to the innocent side. The team gaining possession can either tap the ball on the ground and play on, kick for touch or, if they are in goal kicking range, kick for goal.

PENALTY KICK: A goal resulting from a penalty kick is worth two points, the same as a conversion after scoring a try.

PENALTY TRY: A penalty try can also be awarded if the referee deems a player has been interfered with while endeavouring to score a try. It's worth four points.

DIFFERENTIAL PENALTY KICK: A differential penalty kick is one awarded for a minor infringement during the scrum. A kick at goal is not allowed from this type of penalty.

KICKING FOR TOUCH

A team can 'kick for touch' to gain extra ground during play. If, for instance, a penalty is awarded but the goal posts are out of range, a well placed kick down-field and over the touchline on the full means that the team in possession can re-start play where the ball crossed the touchline.

In general play a kick for touch is slightly different: the ball must bounce inside the touchline. If it goes over on the full, play will restart with a scrum feed to the opposition, or a handover if it was on the last tackle, at the point where the kick was taken. A kick for touch that stays in the field of play will still result in the opponents gaining possession but the team that kicked gains valuable territory. If, however, the ball touches an opposition player before it crosses the touchline then the kicking team will gain the advantage of territory and possession.

EXTRAS

SEND OFF: Deliberate breaking of the rules can result in being sent from the field, thereby leaving your team one man down for the rest of the match. A follow-up appointment with the judiciary is a certainty.

SIN BIN: Lesser offences, such as arguing with the ref, picking fights and a bad attitude, result in a sin binning – ten minutes on the sideline, leaving your team one man short for the duration.

OFFSIDE: Simply put, an attacking player must be either in line with or behind the team mate with the ball if he expects to receive it. If he is in front of his team mate and receives the ball a penalty is awarded to the opposing team.

The other key application of the offside rule concerns kicking. If team mates are in front of a player kicking the ball they must remain at least 10 metres away from the opponent receiving the ball; anyone inside this territory cannot tackle the opponent. And at the restart of play, players on the team kicking off must remainbehind the halfway line until the kick is taken. An infringement of this results in a penalty to the opposition.

REPLACEMENT RULE: During a game a coach can substitute or replace up to four players with reserves from the bench. However, a total of six substitutions can be made during a game using a combination of the reserves and resting players who are already on the field.

BLOOD BIN: Any bleeding player must leave the field to have the wound attended to and can be replaced without it being counted as one of the six substitutions. It's basically a free substitution.

HALF TIME

As soon as the ref whistles halftime, or the siren has blown, the teams charge off the ground and into their dressing rooms for a memorable speech from the coach.

Opinion is still divided over whether the coach's pearls are being thrown before swine or whether his impassioned plea has some effect.

Meanwhile the crowd is entertained in two ways. The women get all teary and feel motherhood swell in their womb as they watch the cute little four year olds playing their mini version of rugby league. It's almost a shame to think of these gorgeous little kids growing up to be battered and bruised first graders, but it's their choice after all, I suppose.

The men are more intrigued by the athletic ability of the cheerleaders who perform cartwheels, backflips and the splits in sequined G-string leotards. Ask any bloke what the girls were wearing though, and he wouldn't be able to tell you; he was simply admiring the gymnastic display, as any good sporting connoisseur would.

SECOND HALF

Much the same as the first half except the teams swap ends. The second half is where you find value for money. The sides are refreshed and motivated; competition is renewed and at full pace again; the crowd has had its fill of halftime banter and a tinny or two and it's basically like seeing a whole new game – two for the price of one. But, wait, there's more...

The teams have regrouped. They've summarised the situation, they know where they stand in this fight for manhood and they've drawn up the battle lines for the last 40 minutes of play. You will

BULLDOZER

This story is based on fact. Only the player's name has been altered to protect their his esteem...

In the late 1980s, a player named Bulldozer was listening to the halftime speech from his coach. The coach was renowned for reciting historical motivational pieces and on this particular day he was reciting the words Winston Churchill used to spur on his soldiers during the war. The coach's impassioned rendition finished with, 'Winston's boys did it for him, now will you do it for me?' To which Bulldozer responded by asking one of his mates, 'Who was Winston? I don't remember him ever playing for this club!'

Perhaps a moist towelette and a sip of orange cordial is all the boys need at halftime.

often notice a change in attitude in the second half. The team that's in front prances out onto the ground like lions emerging from their den, while the losing team thunders out like elephants with a mission: too big, too fast, too powerful to be thrown off the scent – they smell victory, but it's a fair way off.

The teams' attitudes are reflected in the crowd. All of a sudden the crowd buzz rises an octave or two – don't be surprised to find yourself screaming at pitches you never realised existed.

By now you've figured out which of the players' bottoms you like, which of the players' legs you fancy and which of the players' shoulders make you weak at the knees. Continue to watch these key figures while you learn more about the game from the way their muscles ripple. But also spend some time analysing what else is going on in the game. Watching the bench is worth a good ten minutes. It helps you gauge the confidence factor. Is the coach the strong, silent type giving nothing away, or is he the ranting and raving type exuding the energy his players need to pull off a win?

THE REFEREES

Rugby league is becoming so fast and strong that it won't be long before the game is deemed too much for one referee to handle. Like other ball sports, such as basketball and netball, a second ref will be brought into the game to patrol one half of the field. The ref does have some assistance, though. His Walkman isn't playing 17th century classics, or the latest Techno Funk track: he's actually wired up to his two touch judges – rule enforcers who run along the touchline ensuring players don't go out of bounds and determining the precise point at which a ball has gone into touch (over the touchline). These little mafia men also keep their eyes on players who may be trying to break the rules of the game. When a fight erupts in back play, touch judges determine who started what and who should be penalised. Everybody loves touch judges.

When a try is scored the touch judges, along with the in-goal judges, determine whether the ball actually hit the ground or whether the player was held up. When an attempt at goal is being made, they stand behind the goal posts. If the kick is successful, they raise their brightly coloured flags in the air, and if the kick was a shocker they wave their flags from side to side at waist level.

The flags themselves are masterpieces. Australian referees' coordinator, Mick Stone, has taken a personal interest in referee accessories since he decided to take charge of this burgeoning industry.

'Traditionally, touch judge flags were supposed to be red and white, but because of rugby league's move towards night games, we wanted something far more stark – now they're iridescent yellow with red and blue pinlines.' It's taken Mick years to coordinate the textures, colours and designs of referee apparel but international sources agree that he's really got it down to perfection. Our linesman's flags are the envy of the world

You have to admire the ref and his two touch judges for their fitness and their concentration – not to mention their obvious psychological challenges. Anybody who willingly walks out onto a field expecting to control two sides of wild beasts obviously considers himself a bit of a Tarzan. What a shame they don't wear a Tarzan loin cloth. Maybe Mick Stone could consider that for his next update.

Succesful goal

REFEREES SIGNALS

Most common signals from referees and linesmen:

SIN BIN: The referee raises both hands and exposes all ten fingers, representing ten minutes in the sin bin for the player guilty of a misdemeanour such as a head high tackle or dangerous play.

FIVE TACKLES: A raised arm with five fingers showing informs the teams that the tackle just made was the fifth and at the next tackle there will be a mandatory handover of the ball.

HANDOVER: A raised arm, similar to five tackles signal, then the referee bends his knees and feigns a passing of the ball

TRY: The referee will blow his whistle and point to the area where the try has been scored. Players, crowds and officials wait in

Sin bin

Five tackles

Handover

anticipation for this signal because the try can't be awarded until the referee confirms it.

PENALTY KICK: A raised arm points to the team that has just won a penalty.

SCRUM: Both arms raised in an arc, with the fingers meeting over the head, indicates a scrum must form for play to continue.

FULLTIME

The referee blows his whistle and it's all over for another week. Now it's time for total team bonding. The ref shakes the hands of his touch judges, the touch judges pat him on the bottom, the players pat them on the head, the winning players cuddle each other, the coach hugs the team, the trainers kiss each other and

Try   **Penalty Kick**   **Scrum**

RUGBY LEAGUE FAN: KIM VAUTIN

Kim Vautin has been through it all – the trials and tribulations of being married to a representative footballer who's gone on to become a media commentator and funny man.

Husband Paul played his best days with the rugby league team people love to hate, Manly. He captained the side to a premiership victory in 1987. He captained Queensland in the State of Origin and he played 13 tests for Australia. Known as 'Fatty', the former front rower now hosts Channel Nine's rugby league Footy Show and has also enjoyed instant coaching success by leading Queensland to a State of Origin win over NSW in 1995.

'Even though I used to follow Manly I actually met Paul at the bank. He never asked me to go and watch him play but I'd go anyway. I'd always been interested in footy as it was part of my upbringing, but once I started seeing Paul my interest became a bit more intense.

'You can follow the game and know what's going on without needing any in-depth understanding of the rules. And just when you think you've got a grasp on the game, they change a rule. After many years of being involved I still don't have a grasp of all the technicalities.

'Above all other codes, I enjoy watching rugby league, especially State of Origin. There's a terrific social scene with footy too - you all go and sit on the hill, chatting away through the game. The kids are all running around, and if the team wins it's terrific cause you all go back to the club and celebrate. But there's also a down side. There's a lot of travel – the guys go away for a night or two, a week or two. Usually the wives and girlfriends stick together while they're away. In early days the women never toured with the men – it was taboo. During the 80s it was as if the men were going off to war and the women had to stay home. That's changed a bit now.

'Being part of the scene is terrific but during the controversial times you can get a bit sick of it. I remember thinking at one stage, when Paul was being overlooked for representative selection, "oh to hell with the lot of you", but in all honesty if it wasn't for football we wouldn't be where we are now. We wouldn't live in the house we live in and our kids wouldn't go to the schools they go to. Overall rugby league's been of great benefit to us.'

the crowd joins the traffic queue to get out of the place. The losing side hang their heads and tramp from the field. The winners huddle together and run a lap of honour waving at the supportive crowd. Radio and television commentators analyse the spectacle as though it's crucial to the survival of mankind and we are given another game to talk about at home or work or at the gym for the week.

Can you imagine what life was like before you became a footyhead? What on earth was there to think about, or worry about or talk about? Glory, glory... we've seen the light!

6 AUSSIE

RULES

A QUICK HISTORY LESSON

For anybody not born in an Australian Rules dominated state, the game is weird, but it is as wonderful as it is weird. For anybody lucky enough to be born in an aussie rules mad state the game is second nature – nothing strange about it at all.

Formerly called Victorian Football, it's been the divisive element between Australia's eastern states (NSW and Qld) and the rest of the country. While rugby league and rugby union are more popular on the east coast, they don't rate a mention in any other part of the country. In fact, most Australians outside NSW and Qld think that union and league are the same game! But we know better, don't we, fellow footyheads?

Strangely enough, it is a New South Welshman who is credited with having developed the game in 1859. Thomas Wills went to England for schooling, and became a top cricketer and rugby player. When he returned to Australia, he settled in Victoria and played cricket for the state. After an embarrassing loss to a NSW side, Wills became convinced that the Victorian cricketers lacked the fitness of their counterparts across the border (some say they still do!). He decided to set in place a training schedule for the cricketers during the off season, and rugby was chosen as a basis. He thought rugby was too strenuous however, so he and a couple of mates started experimenting – adopting ideas from all over the world as well as coming up with a few of their own. At about the same time a schoolmaster from Scotch College in Melbourne, a former student and rugby player in England, had half a dozen rugby balls sent out from the mother country for his pupils to play with. Together with the schoolboys, these gentlemen effectively invented a game in which the rules were – there are no rules! What was actually being played was a cocktail of sport – ideas were taken from Gaelic football (played by the Irish miners in the area), soccer and rugby, with a few other herbs and spices thrown in to create this unique new game.

The first AFL club, Melbourne, was started in 1859. The early games lasted for days – play only stopping when the teams needed a drink. The winning side was the first to get two goals ahead. With up to 40 players in a team, managing a two goal break was extremely difficult and often games that began in the morning were no nearer to being finalised even by sunset.

Because the game was designed for cricketers, it was cricket ovals where the first contests took place. To this day aussie rules is played on vast, oval-shaped grounds rather than on the rectangular fields of other football codes. Given the size of the playing area there are more players per team (18) than in any other code.

It quickly developed into a fast, furious game which attracted the support of players' families and friends and overtook all other codes as our premier football game.

At the turn of the century there were discussions about merging aussie rules with rugby league. But due to lack of interest, or that friendly rivalry that still exists between the states, both codes remained sacred to their own territory… and with it survived a game that is purely ours.

Aussie rules' beginnings were very much focussed in Victoria, but as the miners of the 1800s spread west and north across the continent, the game, so much a part of their lives in Victoria, went with them. Now every State and Territory in Australia has its own competition, as well as the national league contested by teams in Victoria, Queensland, New South Wales, South Australia and Western Australia.

Aussie rules appears to have been ahead of its footballing counterparts in many ways. It beat the other codes in Australia in turning professional, way back in 1897, although the news wasn't made public and official until 1911. While many of the players are full-time professionals these days, there are still some clubs battling to make ends meet and their players work either full or part-time. David Parkin, one of the league's top coaches, has been involved with lucrative, glamour clubs during his career but still advises players to have an alternative form of work outside of football. He believes sport is all about passion and emotion and it's pretty difficult to feel passionate and emotional about something you live and breathe 24 hours a day.

Unlike other codes women have always played a part in the game, Soccer, rugby union and rugby league were the bastions of men for many years, only recently accepting women as a valued part of the game – whether it be as players, coaches or spectators. In aussie rules, though, women were a large part of the audience as far back as the turn of the century – they made up a large part of the crowd at most games and in 1902, one sixth of the season ticket holders at Collingwood were female.

With the introduction of global television, and pay TV, aussie rules today is seen by millions of viewers around the world. Competitions are even played in the USA, England, Canada, Denmark, Asia and in small island nations like Nauru. As far back as 1908 New Zealand brought a team to Australia for a promotional tour.

WHAT THE GAME IS
ALL ABOUT

Aussie rules is about being unique – the game is, the players are, even the grounds are. Unlike other sports there are no set dimensions for the ground. However, a length of between 150 and 185 metres and a width of 130 to 150 metres is recommended. Goal kicking is also unique, because even if you miss, you can still earn a point. Scoring is unique – instead of having Collingwood beating Richmond 96-70, the score would read Collingwood 13.18.96, Richmond 10.10.70: Collingwood winning by 26 points.

The aim of the game is to score more points than the opposition. In doing this, the game of aussie rules is a frenzied activity and has fewer stoppages than any other code of football. The emphasis is on speed, accuracy, strength and agility. While rugby league and rugby union have a reputation of being the tough, gritty games, aussie rules is as rough as you can get: players walk all over team mates and opponents alike, deliberately bumping into players without the ball is allowed, and groping hands can be dangerous in any situation. Yet, because there is no send-off rule in the AFL, the game rolls on and the unsuspecting spectator may not realise just how many collisions and damaged bodies have been racked up during a game. There is no offside rule either, but nor is there brawling! So what are all of those punch-ups you see so frequently? They are called 'melees'. One of the rules in aussie rules is that no more than four players are allowed in each melee. Why don't they just ban melees? While the umpire can't send off any trouble makers, he is free to report them at the end of the game, which results in a trip to the Monday night tribunal hearing. Video evidence can be played at the tribunal and most melee instigators find themselves suspended for a week or two, depending on the severity of their behaviour.

CENTRE SQUARE

In the middle of the field is the centre square, measuring 45 square metres. The centre square is used each time the game is restarted: at the beginning of each quarter or after a goal has been scored. Only four players from each side are allowed in this area: usually the ruckman, ruck rover, rover and centreman.

CENTRE CIRCLE

At the heart of the centre square is the centre circle, measuring 3 metres in diameter. At the start, and each restart, the field umpires bounce the ball in the centre circle. Each team's ruckman then contests the 'knock-out', the successful ruckman knocking the ball towards one of his team mates to get the show on the road.

GOAL POSTS

There are four posts located on the boundary line at each end of the ground. There are 6.4 metres between each post, the two centre posts are the goalposts, about 6 metres in height, while the two outside posts are the behind posts and measure about 3 metres in height.

A goal is worth six points and is scored by kicking an untouched ball between the two goalposts. If the ball is touched by a player, or it hits one of the posts, it is registered as a behind,

AFL FIELD AND DIMENSIONS

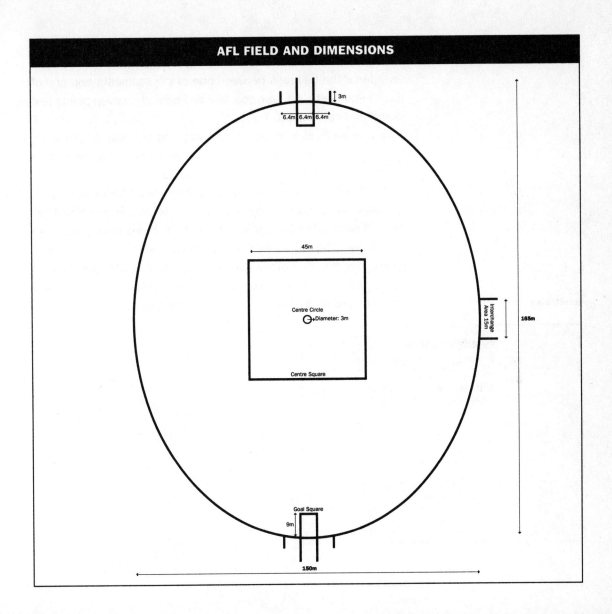

worth one point. It's also deemed a behind if it is scored by a defending player (similar to an own goal in soccer). A behind is awarded if the ball rolls between one of the goalposts and one of the behind posts. So, one goal and one behind = seven points and is written like this: 1.1.7.

If a team is kicking well on the day and put both of the kicks through for goal they would then have two goals, no behinds, and 12 points which is written like this: 2.0.12.

Goals are preferable, obviously, but behinds often win a game.

While some football codes pride themselves on technicalities, AFL followers pride themselves on their six times table. You need an honours degree in maths to keep score in an aussie rules game. It is this fact alone that has been responsible for most of our Melbourne business executives finding international success in the corporate world. They know their maths!

Result card

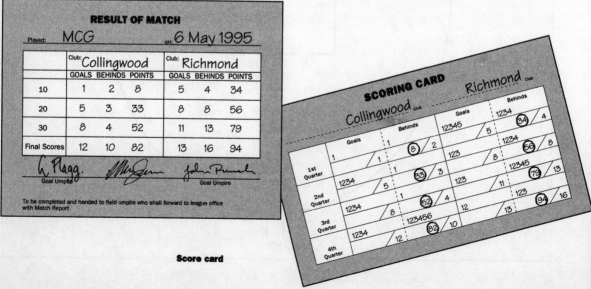

RESULT OF MATCH

Played: MCG   on: 6 May 1995

	Club: Collingwood			Club: Richmond		
	GOALS	BEHINDS	POINTS	GOALS	BEHINDS	POINTS
10	1	2	8	5	4	34
20	5	3	33	8	8	56
30	8	4	52	11	13	79
Final Scores	12	10	82	13	16	94

G. Flagg.

Goal Umpire   John Punch   Goal Umpire

To be completed and handed to field umpire who shall forward to league office with Match Report

Score card

SCORING CARD

Collingwood Club   Richmond Club

		Collingwood				Richmond		
		Goals	Behinds		Goals	Behinds		
1st Quarter		1	1	(8) / 2	12345	1234	(34) / 4	
			1	(33) / 3	123	1234	(56) / 8	
2nd Quarter		1234	5 : 1	(52) / 4	123	12345	(79) / 13	
3rd Quarter		1234	8 : 123456	(82) / 10	12	123	(94) / 16	
4th Quarter		1234	12		13			

GOAL SQUARE

I warned you about aussie rules being a strange game: the goal square is a rectangle! It's an area that stretches 9 metres out from the goalposts and is used by the full backs to restart play with a kick-out after a behind has been scored. The goal square was the hot-spot for clashes between full forwards, aiming to kick goals, and full backs, aiming to stop them, but these days the strength and accuracy of the kicking game means a lot of the action takes place well outside the goal square area.

UNDERSTANDING THE TIME

Each game has four quarters, each supposedly of 20 minutes duration. At the end of each quarter, however, time-on is added for any stoppages in play. The two time keepers, one from each team, record the amount of time taken to restart the game after a goal, to recover a ball that is out of play, or for breaks due to player injury. The total of all stoppages is then played at the end of the 20 minute quarter, which ends up being about a 28 minute quarter.

Halftime is 20 minutes (spent with the coach in the dressing room). At quarter and three quarter time teams huddle on the edge of the ground discussing share prices and weather for five minutes.

THE PLAYERS

Another aspect unique to aussie rules is the variety of physiques required for the game. The rugby codes generally suit smaller, heavier players with a low centre of gravity because most of the game is played close to the ground. In the Australian game, however, you need slim, trim basketball star look-alikes to control that part of the game played in the air, while your smaller, dashing speedsters pick up stray balls and fulfil the roving requirements.

Watching a team of players spill onto the ground is like pouring open a Christmas stocking. You never know what's next. There are big ones, little ones, cute ones, sweet ones and ones that you would probably be better off without.

All of them though have bodies to die for. If they were horses you could back them in any field – they run, they jump, they kick and boy, can they flex! Their arms are chiselled to perfection and their legs are streamlined for speed and distance.

The taller players are suited to the key positions of full forward or fullback, where getting airborn to catch the ball (or to take a mark) is all important. They need their size for distance kicking too. Smaller players are the rovers, and the ruck rovers, who must be agile and creative. Here are the 18 positions:

FULL FORWARD: Placed right in front of the open mouth goal to score as often as possible. They are the heroes of the team and receive more fan mail than the tax man receives returns. Best examples are Gary Ablett (also known as God) and Tony Locket, two of the AFL's most famous names.

LEFT FORWARD POCKET: Sits in full forward's left pocket and collects any fan mail spilt. Acts as a back-up goal kicking machine for the full forward.

RIGHT FORWARD POCKET: Same as left forward pocket except on the other side of the ground.

CENTRE HALF FORWARD: Midway between open mouth goal and centre circle. These crucial players must win the ball and then deliver it into the hands of the goal kickers. If they are in position they may kick for goal themselves. Often the best looking players on the ground. Best examples are Wayne Carey and Steven Kernahan.

LEFT HALF FORWARD FLANK: Resides in centre half forward's left pocket and plays second fiddle to him.

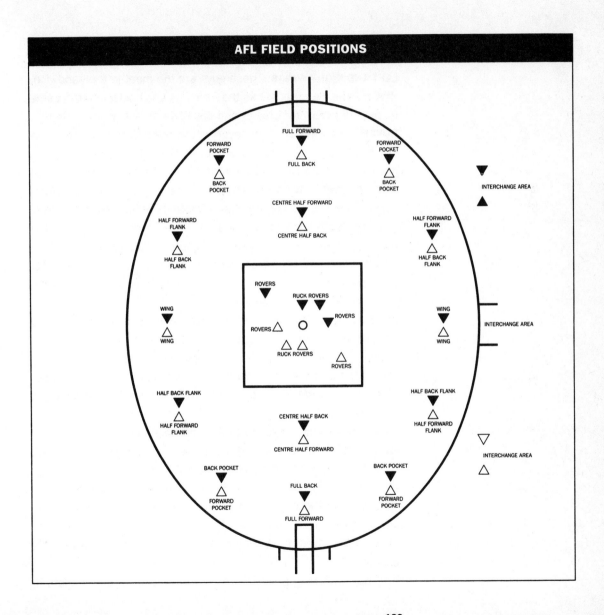

AFL FIELD POSITIONS

RIGHT HALF FORWARD FLANK: Another back-up for the centre half forward, but on the other side of the ground.

LEFT AND RIGHT WINGS: These guys are the meat in the sandwich, they are the glue that sticks the forwards and backs into the same game. They hunt for breaks and capitilise on every opportunity.

ROVER: The prowler – the everywhere man. Rovers are usually small and dangerous like scorpions. They like to play in traffic jams and can be counted on to appear at the most crucial times.

RUCK ROVERS (OR FOLLOWERS): Each team has two ruck rovers who are the thinkers on the team. Captains are suited to this role. They are the hitmen of any side – they're called in to put out the fires, and then they leave. Best example is Paul Kelly.

CENTRE: Winning centre bounces is of primary importance. After that, directing play and anticipating movement are key roles. Watch out for Greg Williams.

CENTRE HALF BACK: Midway between centre circle and opposition's goal mouth. Crucial line of defence – if the opposition breaks through, they are into goal scoring territory.

LEFT HALF BACK FLANK: Another crucial defensive position but must have degree of creativity to capitilise on opponent's mistakes.

RIGHT HALF BACK FLANK: Ditto left half back flank.

FULL BACK: right in the middle of the opposition's open mouth goal. Tall, tough, afraid of nobody, full of hope. Expert spoiler [see glossary].Take note of Steven Silvani's on-field performances.

LEFT BACK POCKET: Strong in defence, support role for full back, sits in the fullback's left pocket.

RIGHT BACK POCKET: You guessed it – sits in the fullback's right pocket.

(Imagine having that many men pouring out of your pockets?)

START THE CLOCK

Before a game of aussie rules begins, the teams must face a tough test to determine whether they are worthy of performing on the sacred turf for the next two and a half hours. As the sides run out onto the park for the game the players must negotiate their way through the banner. An aussie rules banner is not some cheap, hurriedly thrown together cardboard cutout, it's a mammoth offering, made by the supporters group each week, to dedicate to the footballing gods, hoping they will shine down on the game and bring success to the chosen players. These banners are a work of art. Often players need more than one attempt to break through. It's more like watching a team of builders trying to break down the wall of a house, than a couple of footballers running through a flag.

Once onto the field, after the mandatory warm-up and stretching routines, one of the field umpires will bounce the ball in the centre circle and the game is under way. The crowd is probably in full chant already, calling for their favourite players to show the

UMPIRE'S BOUNCE

An umpire will bounce the ball several times during a game to get play back underway. Some of the most common occasions are:

- *Start play at the beginning of each quarter*
- *Re-start play after a goal has been kicked*
- *When a mark is contested by opposing players*
- *Disperse scrimmages*

Bounce

rest of the world why aussie rules is such a special game. The ruckman from each team will jump for the ball hoping to knock it to their rovers. The aim is to keep it moving quickly down towards your forwards who can take a mark and kick for goal.

Once a goal is kicked, the game is restarted with another centre bounce. If a behind is kicked, the opposition's full back will restart the game by kicking the ball from the goal square.

A player can run with the ball, providing he **bounces** it once every 15 metres. While this sounds like an easy task, it takes a great deal of expertise and constant practice. Just to add a bit of personal experience, why don't you go grab a ball, any kind of ball, and run down the hallway or the backyard, at full pace, bouncing and catching the ball, without interrupting your Melinda Gainsford type rhythm. Go on, don't read any further until you've done it!

How did you go? It's not that easy is it? Now, whenever you see a game of aussie rules, you will appreciate precisely how talented the players are – making difficult skills look so easy and fluid.

When the opportunity, or necessity, to pass to a team mate arises, there is one of two choices – handball or kick.

Handball

HANDBALL

Throwing is not permitted. To handball, the ball is held in one hand and punched away with the other – like a volleyball serve. Some players get confused and hold a player with one hand while punching him with the other – this isn't a handball, it's a melee. Players sometimes find it difficult not to get the two confused!

THE KICK

There are two main kicks used in aussie rules, although there are a number of others used in special circumstances.

The drop punt is the most common because of its accuracy. The ball is dropped onto the toe of the kicking foot and booted so that it spins end-over-end. The torpedo is used mostly for distance. The ball is held at a slight angle so when it's kicked it spins in a spiral, rather than end-over-end.

Next time you're in the local park playing with the kids and you boot a pathetic, dribbling ball about 10 centimetres in front of you, stop and take note. Then when you're watching your next aussie

FREE KICKS

Common reasons for free kicks:

- *Holding the man*
- *Holding the ball*
- *Charging*
- *Kicking in danger*
- *Kicking out of bounds of the field*
- *Tackling above the shoulder*
- *Pushing in the back*

Kicking

AUSSIE RULES FAN (NOT!): CHERYL BARASSI

Anybody looking for a bit of backup or an excuse to put this book down and never have anything to do with football again – look no further! You've found a partner in Cheryl Barassi. Here's your one and only offer for an alibi...

Married to one of the true legends of aussie rules, Cheryl says it doesn't mean she's had to follow the game, be interested in the game or in fact know anything at all about the game. Husband Ron has been involved in football for over 40 years, as player, captain and coach and is perhaps the most famous player of the code. If you were to study the history of AFL clubs Melbourne, Carlton, North Melbourne and the Sydney Swans, the linking thread would be Ron Barassi. He's had a hand in the premiership wins of 1955, '56, '57, '59, '60 and '64.

Despite the game being such a large part of her husband's life, Cheryl freely admits that when she went to her first game with Ron she knew nothing about Aussie Rules. She proudly declares she still doesn't!

'The truth is, it CAN be avoided. I've been with Ron for 20 years, and after my first few stupid remarks at footy games people stopped talking to me about it. It's that easy!

'Last year I was the President's guest at Essendon or somewhere and I saw all this action on the field so I started shouting "C'mon Sydney", until somebody pointed out that the game hadn't started yet.'

Cheryl chose well in picking her husband, because despite Ron's fascination and obvious talents for Aussie Rules, he is involved in many other aspects of life. He enjoys politics, the theatre, current affairs, reading biographies and having rather deep, meaningful conversations with a broad range of dinner guests.

'In 20 years of social gatherings I've never heard Ron talk about footy because he's interested in too many other things. But once he's at a game, you could bite his nose off and he wouldn't realise you were there. I went once and saw the back of his head for the entire match – he didn't talk to me once, wasn't the slightest bit interested in what I was thinking. I decided then and there that that was the last time I would ever go to the footy with him.'

And it was.

The one dilemma Cheryl faces in all of this is that it's mandatory to follow a football club if you live in Victoria. But she's found away around that...

'Oh, yes, you can be bashed for not supporting a team. I quickly aligned myself with St Kilda because nobody cares if you follow them. Now when anybody asks who I support, I just say 'The Saints' and that ends the conversation!'

rules match, just stand in awe of what the players can do with one ball and one foot. Kicking a goal with pinpoint accuracy from 70 metres out makes spectators drool with admiration. The power involved, the precision…it makes your mind wander. What would you do if you had that sort of power and precision? No longer would you have to carry the rubbish bins out – you could merely drop punt them from home to the city tip; never again would you have to carry the shopping from the supermarket to the carpark – you could just belt it from the checkout into the boot; and the kids – they could be drop punted from bed into the bath, from the bathroom to the kitchen and from the kitchen straight to the playground at school!

Other forms of kicking are: the drop kick (an unfashionable form of kick also used to describe unfashionable people), the banana kick (which curves), and the flat punt (which isn't too accurate and is difficult to mark).

THE BALL

In the very early days of aussie rules the game was predominantly played with a round ball. Even though early experimentation began with rugby balls in 1859, it wasn't until 1880 that the oval-shaped ball was adopted.

Since then the only major change has been a scaling down in the size – while rugby balls have a circumference of around 775mm x 600mm, aussie rules balls measure 725mm x 550mm.

While it's the ball that commands most of the attention in any game of football, there's also a heck of a lot of action occuring away from the ball. Downfield in the forward pocket there's jostling between the protagonists looking for a physical and mental edge over their opponent, even though the ball might still

---

50 METRE PENALTY

For secondary infringements, a 50 metre penalty can be awarded whereby the non-offending team can move 50 metres nearer to the opponents goal.

Such infringements include:

- *Failing to comply with the umpire's directions*
- *Depriving an opponent of the ball*
- *Encroaching over the mark where a free kick is to be taken*
- *Wasting time*
- *Disputing umpires decision*

be 100 metres away. A lot of the action centres on one-on-one marking, like in basketball. The challenge is to elude your opponent and find the space to lure the ball out of the hands of an aware team mate and into your own. That quick elbow, a lightning shove, followed by a dash away from the opposition will give you space, and with the space comes crucial breaks that can win you the game. Many such crucial breaks come with a successful mark.

THE MARK

A mark is a catch taken from the kick of a team mate not less than 10 metres away. A successful mark gives the player some breathing space – he's free to play on, handball, or if in position, kick for goal.

Marking is one of the most spectacular components of an aussie rules game. All of a sudden those thundering, muscular machines become human torpedoes, launching into the air to stop the flight of the ball as though it's an enemy jet-fighter. Michael Jordan reckons he's a hit leaping to the basketball rim for a slam dunk, well, let me tell you, Air Jordan's got nothing on an AFL mark. Players dive for marks, jump for marks, and leap for marks – and every kind will get your heart pumping!

TACKLING

Any player with the ball can be tackled between the knees and the shoulders provided he isn't pushed from behind. Unlike rugby league play doesn't usually stop after a tackle. The minute a player is tackled, he must dispose of the ball. Because of this non-stop action, and the number of players on the ground, there are plenty of opportunities for the ball to go astray or for an

Taking a mark

opponent to intercept as the tackled player struggles to kick or handball quickly to a team mate. It's this quality that makes aussie rules one of the most heart-stopping and unpredictable games on earth.

If a tackled player has a reasonable chance to release the ball but does not do so, a free kick will be awarded to the opposition. If it's physically impossible for a tackled player to dispose of the ball, the umpire will restart the game with a bounce.

In soccer, rugby union and league it's illegal to interfere with any player other than the one with the ball; in aussie rules it's not. Shepherding plays a large part in the game. Players can push or shove opponents off the ball as they strive for possession, they can use their hips, hands and shoulders to check opponents within five metres of the ball, they can shield a team mate by standing in front of a charging opponent, they can even start a melee if they so desire – as long as they remember, no more than four players allowed at the one party!

There is so much that happens in a single game of aussie rules – it's a real festival of gamesmanship and athleticism. Listening to a game on radio will wear you out, it's almost impossible to keep up with the call. Watching a game on TV will also consume you, but nothing matches the exhilaration of actually being there. Make an effort to get to a game of aussie rules as soon as you can. Having gone once, promise yourself you will go again because it takes quite a few visits to the local ground before you have the capacity to absorb everything that's happening in the game.

The atmosphere will grab you from the first instant. The crowd is electric. The hooters are sounding, like a warning siren at a train station letting you know the next express is only moments

Tackle

away. The teams storm onto the oval like a troupe of circus dancers, they crash through the banner and they're ready to go. aussie rules is absorbing – don't let anybody tell you otherwise.

THE UMPIRES

There are seven umpires per game. Three field umpires, one for each half of the ground to control the action and another to keep an overall eye on things, two boundary umpires to keep watch on balls going outside the boundary lines, and two goal umpires to signal goals, behinds or no-goals.

The fashion gurus are the goal umpires, who wear nice white bowling hats and long-sleeved white coats over black pants. They even wear ties. They carry lovely large white flags which they wave when one of their favourite players kicks a goal or a behind. The signal for goal is along the lines of Quick Draw McGraw pulling a gun out of each pocket and firing simultaneously. Bent at the elbow, the umpires' arms shoot out with his index fingers pointing straight ahead. Then the umpire grabs his flags from their pouch on the goal post, and he waves frantically, while the goal umpire at the opposite end of the ground mirrors his action. To signal a behind it's much easier – the John Wayne one gun approach, followed by the one-flag-wave.

If you're a real footyhead, next time you go to an aussie rules game one of the really cool things to do is sit behind the goal posts in your home-knitted beanie and scarf and copy the umpires' movements. When he signals goal, you signal goal. When he signals a behind, you signal a behind. Gee it's fun.

Goal umpires are also charged with keeping a running tally of the score. During each quarter they pencil in every goal and behind scored by each side. At the end of the game they add up

Goal

Behind

the scores, sign their cards, and hand them to the field umpire. The field umpire then adds his match report, detailing any naughty players who will need to make a date with the tribunal, and together they are handed to the AFL officials.

When you were at school, do you remember playing 'Queenie, Queenie, who's got the ball?' Well that game was actually started by AFL boundary umpires. Their sole duty is to whistle the field umpires every time a ball goes over the boundary line and out of bounds. Play is stopped while the boundary umpire retrieves the ball, turns his back to the players, and throws the ball over his head, known as a throw-in. The waiting ruckmen then wrestle for the ball.

If the ball is kicked out of bounds on the full, the opposing team receives a free kick at the spot where the ball crossed the line.

There is also an emergency field umpire who watches out for MLMs – *Men Looking for Melees*. The emergency umpire can dart onto the field at any time to reprimand MLMs but cannot participate in the decision-making part of the game.

COACHES

AFL coaches are the most advanced of all football codes in Australia. They don't sit on the edge of the field, or near the interchange bench, like other codes they have private boxes, away from the screaming crowds and prying television cameras. They relay messages via walky-talky or mobile phone to their trainers who are seen weaving through the game for its entirety.

Goal

Coaches also have a messenger, called a runner, whose sole job is to relay messages from coach to players. They develop diplomatic skills worthy of a position in the United Nations. They also wear conspicuous lime green uniforms.

AUSSIE RULES PLAYER: JUNE LUFF

June Luff gained notoriety as a top ruck before needing a total knee reconstruction after a game in 1983. Her son Troy now plays aussie rules and has gained some notoriety of his own as a strong-marking utility. June's footballing career was mostly a social one – for the Catrick Crescent Cuties, a team that played a couple of matches a season in Traralgon, a town famous for producing top quality aussie rules players.

'We even played as the warm-up to the main men's games a couple of times, we took ourselves pretty seriously. We drew quite a good crowd, we weren't laughed at or anything because, gee, in Victoria football is football – it doesn't matter who plays it!'

Without revealing her age, June says she played for years before the injury forced retirement. She'd give her eye teeth, though, to be able to play today.

'I was born at the wrong time. There are girls playing in boys teams at school, these days. When I was at school we weren't allowed to play with the boys, but we'd go off and play our own games. I belonged to the Police Boys & Citizens Youth Club so we got to play there, but because half of the girls were better than the boys, they used to get cheesed off and throw us in the mud after the games just to let us know what 'real' footy was all about! Oh, I just loved it.'

When the Traralgon Jubilee newspaper had a special edition, celebrating 20 years of football in the area, June was written up along with some of the big names of the game such as Bernie Quinlan and Neil Cordy. But she says the women's games were always treated as a bit of a novelty in Victoria. In NSW it is quite different.

'We moved to the north coast of NSW in the heart of rugby territory. There's a women's team that plays touch and they are taken very seriously. It surprised me. I'm still trying to work out why women's football can be taken seriously in one State, but not in another.'

Despite June's experience and longevity in the game, her son is reluctant to take advice from his mum. 'I've been watching him play since he was 7, and I still bite my nails down to the cuticles at every game. Every time I talk to him on the phone I try to pass on a bit of advice and tell him how to play the game but he doesn't think I know anything. I suppose I'm still considered a bit of a novelty – not to be taken too seriously!'

At quarter, and three quarter time, the coach and staff gather in the team huddle on the boundary line to discuss tactics. At half time they all retreat to the dressing rooms for a 20 minute dressing down. It would be wonderful to be a fly on the wall at one of these halftime meetings because often the side that runs back onto the field for the second half of the game is different to the one that left the same field 20 minutes earlier. You will be able to gauge the worth of your team's coach by watching for this. If your team comes back looking like they haven't had a break, the coach needs to go. If they come bounding back out like Easter bunnies delivering chocolate eggs, your coach is worth his salt.

UNDERSTANDING THE HOOTER

You can't. I'm convinced all hooters and sirens are for atmosphere only. Hooters sound before play, to start play, to stop play each quarter, during each quarter, at the end of the game and well and truly after the game. The best idea is to wear your own watch and keep an eye on the umpire – that way you need never try to fathom how there can be so many sirens in one game of football.

Now, go and enjoy it

7 NOT FOR

JUST BLOKES

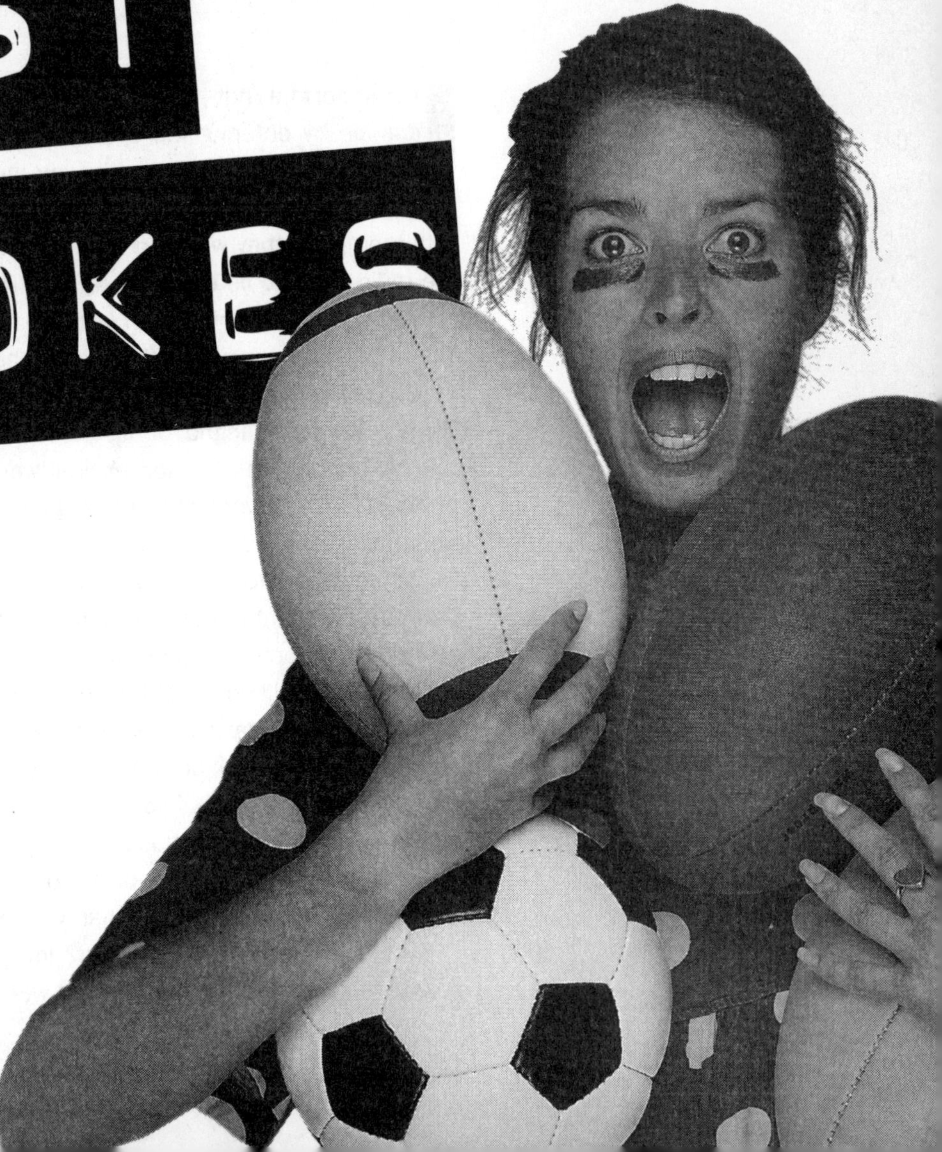

It's important not to feel that you are intruding on man's domain by entering the big, bold world of footy. While some blokes will feel threatened by you moving into their 'territory', most guys will love it – you can share a major part of their lives with them, and they will stop feeling guilty every time they turn on the radio or TV to listen to yet ANOTHER game of football.

There are plenty of women involved in footy on a regular basis. These days women run football clubs, they market the game, they manage players, they coach, they play and some even referee the game. Sweden's Ingrid Jonsson became the first woman to referee an international soccer final when she was given charge of the Germany versus Norway game at the Women's World Championships in 1995.

Women seem to have a natural leadership quality which means they can march into foreign territory, have a quick scout around to see what's happening, then launch a pretty convincing takeover bid. The same will no doubt happen in sport on a worldwide scale, and that trend is starting now! Realise that you are part of the act and that the script can be written any way you like . . . write yourself into the coaching staff of your local team, write yourself onto the board of your nearest national league team or get into the publicity department for the next World Cup campaign and make footy a bigger part of your life than your boyfriend's or husband's!

Wouldn't that be a turnaround? Imagine the guys in your life asking you what you think about next week's match? You can start spurting out the ifs and buts they normally carry on with! And it's a hell of a lot more enjoyable sprouting than being sprouted at. Give it a go.

A lot of people who have no idea about football end up becoming hooked by simply offering to coach the local kid's side. It's a great way to learn, because you are learning as the kids do, as well as making the same mistakes first up, but because of the personal experience, you end up with a deeper understanding of the game than by just reading the rule book. You really must experience the sensation of booting a ball off the inside of your foot, the outside of your foot, your head, your thigh and any other moveable part of your body (except your hands, of course, if you're playing soccer!).

Women's teams exist in all four major codes. There is competition around Australia in aussie rules, rugby league, rugby union and soccer with the Australian women's soccer team ranked right up there with the world's best. In fact, they are even a medal chance when the Olympics roll around in the year 2000.

Outside of the four major codes there are various codes of mixed footy – touch football and Oztag, for example, which are booming. There are competitions throughout Australia played either on weekends or midweek evenings and they provide a fantastic atmosphere for girlfriends/boyfriends, husbands/wives, brothers/sisters to get together, have a bit of fun and learn a few footballing secrets while they're at it.

Basically the idea is to have a bit of fun. If you want to go on and become an 'elite' player, there's room for that, but most people join a footy team to get involved in all the extra-curricula activities. And after all, there's no social scene that rivals football's social scene.

My beautician is one of those eternally slim, feminine, good-

OZTAG

OZTAG is a new national sport with its foundations based on rugby league.

The game was invented four years ago by former league player Perry Haddock. He decided a form of non-contact rugby league should be developed as a training game for his under-21 team. The game was quickly adopted by women, men and children around the country.

Oztag has had a growth rate of 40% per year since its inception. After spreading throughout Australia it has also moved offshore to New Zealand. The game is now played at a regional, state and national level.

looking types with perfect makeup and nails 24 hours a day. I bet if you called around to her place at about 3am and woke her, she'd still look like Cinderella – absolutely perfect. Anyway, in trying to distract me from the pain of a bikini wax one afternoon, she told me she'd joined the local women's soccer comp. I laughed and told her my pain wasn't all that bad, she didn't have to lie.

'No, seriously, I joined without knowing anyone or any of the rules, but I scored a goal in my first game and now I'm hooked!'

Football is that easy. It's not like spiders and snakes and all the other gruesome things boys like – it's actually very enjoyable. It sure beats the repetition of power walking, and it's a lot more fun than having bikini waxes.

WOMEN'S SOCCER

The number one sport in the world is soccer. The World Cup is held once every four years and attracts television audiences in the billions. It's the only sporting event in the world that challenges the Olympics. Now the women's game has its own World Cup, and from 1996 it will also be a medal sport at the Olympics.

But while professional men's contracts around the world are worth millions of dollars, and are fought in courtrooms more often than boardrooms, spare a thought for Australian women players.

The national women's team had its airfares paid to Brazil, for a World Cup warm-up tournament, but had to fork out for everything else – accommodation, food, laundry, travel, etc. Representing your country can be an expensive hobby!

The Australian women's team is captained by Julie Murray, who played professionally in Denmark for two years before coming home to spend more time with our girls in the buildup to the 1995 World Cup.

Julie picked up the game because her two brothers were constantly kicking a ball around the back yard. Until the age of 12 she played in boys' teams. The boys used to try and kick her in the shins because they couldn't believe a girl could dribble and pass so successfully but that attitude changed during the '80s.

Julie says women's soccer is going through a boom period with development officers travelling through schools, funding being given to state and national teams and more exposure for the national side. All of this helps build an interest and a belief in other women that they can do it too.

'Being an Olympic sport has also really helped. Now that there's more exposure, I think girls are going to want to play soccer more than any other game, because it IS the world game, and it's just so exciting.'

The Australian captain offers this hint for improving your understanding of soccer: 'Aside from actually going to games in Australia, I watch a lot of the Italian League and English League on SBS-TV because the European skills are different from the Australian skills, and it helps broaden your understanding of the game.'

While our women's team is making its move up the international rankings, they still aren't as well off as some other sports – basketball, for instance. Australian basketballers generally have their own sponsors and receive funding, but the Australian soccer team had to pay all its own expenses on a seven week tour of Brazil and Europe.

'Having to work really hard as well as train a couple of times a day gets a bit tiring, but you just have to save, save, save in order to afford the trips away. I'm not complaining, though, because being able to play for your country, let alone captain it, is just a

RUGBY UNION FAN: CARISSA DALWOOD

Champion Australian netballer, Carissa Dalwood, is in a rare situation – while she's playing representative netball, her fiance Richard Tombs is busy on the rugby union field.

'It's funny when Richard comes to watch me play. All of a sudden there's a rugby player sitting in the crowd and getting involved in my game. People are so used to seeing all the wives together at football, but at the netball all the husbands sit together and have their little social scene, and it look quite funny.

'When we come home he starts sharing his point of view on the match – about who played well and who didn't. Even though he's pretty knowledgeable about the game now, he doesn't always get it right.'

Carissa grew up in a sports – mad family in Victoria and South Australia. She played athletics, basketball and netball. Her dad played lacrosse, her mum played netball and her brother, all sports. As far as football was concerned, Carissa was fed a diet of aussie rules.

'I'd never seen rugby league or union before I moved to NSW. I was so used to seeing AFL – either on TV or going to the games at the MCG. But since meeting Richard I'm learning, slowly. Rugby is such a different game, though, it takes a while to adapt.

'When I go to the games I still get more carried away in chatting with the people around me than watching the actual game. My aim for this year is to concentrate a little bit harder and learn more about the game. It's really embarrassing when Richard talks about the match afterwards and I have to admit I didn't actually see most of the moves!

'All sports are the same, though, as far as the social scene goes. The biggest part of any sport is to enjoy it, whether as a player or a spectator. I prefer team sports because there're so many people involved that it's easy to make friendships that can last a lifetime.

'I'm looking forward to sitting down with Richard in 20 to 30 years time and reminiscing about our sporting careers , but at the monment we're still pretty full on training and playing.'

great thrill.' One shock admission from Julie is that the women actually behave in much the same way as the men on tour!

'Well if you're on a four or five week tour, living in hotel rooms out of one suitcase,and just playing and training, playing and training, the stress level starts to build up.

'You really have to have some down time to just kick

back...when we were in Sweden it was one of the girls' birthdays, so we tied her to a tree in the carpark and left her there in the cold for about half an hour while we threw things like cake and mayonnaise at her. 'If you didn't do things like that you'd just go insane!'

Sounds like the team might be slightly insane already.

WOMEN'S RUGBY UNION

After soccer, it is women's rugby union that is making an international mark.

There have been two Women's World Cup Rugby Tournaments although Australia hasn't been represented in either. It seems a shame that in a country which is so football mad, and with our men always ranking amongst the world's best, our women's teams haven't made centre stage yet. Change isn't far away, though. At the last three National Championships for women, team entries have gone from three to 18 with the game now properly organised in almost every Australian state.

Australia regularly plays against New Zealand and there is talk of Canada making a tour soon. Rugby has always been regarded as a game for professionals – not professional players but professional business people. With more women climbing the corporate ladder there are more women who want to get involved in the game, and women's teams are springing up around the world. New Zealand is at the forefront, but Australia isn't far behind.

Established competitions operate out of Queensland, NSW and Western Australia, with the other states involved to lesser degrees. A lot of the teams are coached, managed and run by men who've had years of experience in the game, and because of their involvement, the women's game is taken seriously by a lot of the guys.

Nicky Wickert is the Australian captain. She was only mildly interested in the sport until one of her friends asked her to come and try a game. She wasn't particularly keen to play, but decided to wander down and have a look. She ended up on the field and hasn't looked back since.

'I never played footy as a kid or anything, but I got involved in touch footy a couple of years ago just by going down to have a look. Then the same thing happened with rugby union.

'Captaining an Australian team is an awesome experience. It makes me really proud and even a little bit daunted!'

Women's teams around Australia often play games either before or after men's club games and organisers are working hard to establish this as the norm rather than the exception. Development officers are also trying to get the game into schools, and as a result there's a fair bit of depth at state and national level now.

'When the guys first see us run out onto the ground the ones that haven't experienced it before sometimes jeer, but they soon see we have the skills and the commitment and it doesn't take long for them to start barracking and getting behind us.

'The reaction all round has been pretty positive, really. Even on our trip to New Zealand we had the same sponsors as the men's teams. Now we have to work at obtaining that for the club and state sides.'

Australian women play Under 19 men's rules, which are mostly designed for greater safety, but there is a campaign to play under full men's rules because that's what other women's teams around the world play under.

As far as being offered contracts to play, Nicky thinks that's still a dream.

'I don't think it will happen in my lifetime, but I hope we are the stepping stone for future generations.

'The profile of the game is definitely being raised, and there are plenty more people playing, but what we need is exposure. It would be great to think women could make a career out of playing football!'

There's plenty of room to get involved in women's rugby union if you'd like to give it a go. Women's rugby is working on a campaign to have all men's clubs operate a women's team as well. If you'd like more information, contact your local men's club.

WOMEN'S RUGBY LEAGUE

A great way to convince the blokes that you know more about footy than they do is to ask them this one trivia question. Guaranteed, they won't know the answer.

Question: *In which year was Australia's first ever national women's rugby league team named?*
Answer: *1995*

Women have been playing the game in small pockets around the country for some time but it was only in 1995 that an Australian team was picked to play New Zealand. The organisation of the women's game has struggled because of lack of support and sponsorship, but with more representative games planned against our trans-Tasman rivals, recognition should increase and the women's game will grow.

Natalie Dwyer is the Australian captain and, like, Julie Murray, she began the sport just messing around in the backyard with her brothers. One of her favourite pastimes now is to bag the boys about the fact that she went on to play for her country and they didn't . . . what a turnaround for the books!

Because there wasn't much women's competition around, Natalie decided to take up refereeing, and she is one of the growing number of women whistle-blowers who decide they can still play an important part in the game even if it isn't as a team member. After a couple of years of ref-ing, a girls' comp started in her local area and she traded her whistle for some playing gear. She hasn't looked back.

One problem that confronts women rugby league players is common to many women's sports.

'A lot of people think we're gay. They can't understand why we'd want to play a full body-contact sport like league,' Natalie says.

'The truth is we just love the game . . . it's not all that different from touch footy which hundreds of thousands of women play. We just add the skill of tackling to the ball skills, and it's pretty much the same.

'In the six years I've been playing, the worst injury I've seen is one broken leg and one broken arm. But on some mornings, after being bashed around a bit, I can hardly walk!'

But that happens in netball too: it's not limited to boys' games!

Natalie gave up playing cricket for Australia to concentrate on playing league for her country, and although she'd love to see the day when women could make as much money out of the game as men, she remains cynical.

'Well, I don't know if I'll ever see that day, but then again, all women's sports started out this way, and look where some of

GRID IRON FAN: DANA JONES

The story of football doesn't seem to vary much around the world. There are degrees of professionalism; there is the need for ultimate dedication and there's the same exhilarating level of enjoyment.

Dana is part of the grid iron scene in America. Their competition is the NFL – the National Football League and she's married to the San Francisco 49'ers legendary tight-end, Brent Jones.

In a competition as tough as the NFL, the average career of a player is three and a half years. Brent has been playing for a decade. He's also got his own TV program, so together with his economics degree he's guaranteed himself a future when his football career is over.

One stark difference between the football scene in Australia, and that in the US, is the social side.

'Families are considered a distraction so we rarely travel with the fellas when they go to away games. The wives don't really get together much, there isn't a very strong social scene. But the 49'ers are probably the best team to be involved with. They host a Christmas Party for the kids every year but there are a lot of couples who don't have kids, so you never see them.

'The wives don't even sit together at games. We just get given any spare tickets so we are seated randomly around the arena. But when I talk to baseball wives they have an entire family section behind the dugout, they have childcare at the stadium and all sorts of things.'

As for Dana's personal life...

'I've been a domestic engineer (wife/mum/cook) since I agreed to be with Brent, although I have a psychology minor. Brent would be more than willing to back me, but since a footballer only plays in the NFL for such a short space of time, I think it's fair for me to make the sacrifice at this stage.

Dana's association with football began from day one. 'I have two older sisters and we were the only girls in about a five mile radius from home. We used to play touch football games with all the little boys in the street and it was such a big thing! My dad played at high school and junior college before having three daughters. He taught us three things – how to fish, fix cars and play football!

'They've developed a football game over here for girls called Powder Puff. The name caused a bit of a stir, but at least women can play it competively in colleges, even though it's not yet a professional game.'

Dana met Brent at a college baseball game and has been his strongest supporter since. 'Even though he's been playing for ten years now, I honestly never get sick of football. To watch him go out on the field and be able to do something he's great at and loves to do, is a rare double that not a lot of people have with their jobs.'

them have got – we have Australian basketballers being paid to play the game here and some even play professionally in Europe.

'I don't know when rugby league will reach those heights, but I guess at least we've made a start.

'The really hard thing is when people laugh or jeer when you're running out to play. They soon realise that we aren't going out there to be halfhearted, though – we give it everything. I think once they see that, they start to appreciate it.'

The next step for women's rugby league is to gain sponsorship and some administrative backup. Some of the girls' sides would like to be able to access the men's market by playing warm-up games in the men's national league, but the men haven't been too keen on that idea yet.

WOMEN'S AUSSIE RULES

Of the four major footy codes Aussie Rules seems to offer the least amount of support for the women's game.

Despite the obvious hurdles and barriers put up along the way, women ARE playing the game, and even umpiring.

Kirsten Tona is an AFL umpire who also found herself in the coaching role. When the East Sydney Under 19 men's side was threatened with extinction, because they couldn't regularly field a team, Kirsten volunteered to take over the reigns and make it work. The job carried plenty of pressure, though, because East Sydney was one of the oldest clubs in Australia, with a 115 year old history behind it. Kirsten HAD to make it survive.

Despite a couple of strange glances, and maybe a chuckle or two from other (male) coaches, East Sydney went on to win the premiership under Kirsten's coaching.

It wasn't really an overnight-success story, though. Kirsten's addiction for football began years ago. 'Being born in Melbourne is all that it takes to be footy mad!'

'There used to be a famous group called the anti-football league, led by Keith Dunstan who was a famous columnist. Every year on Grand Final day he and his league would refuse to have anything to do with the footy, so they'd go on a picnic at Hanging Rock. Everyone else in Melbourne hoped that the myth of Hanging Rock would prove itself, and the group would disappear! Unless you were in Keith's anti-football league, you grew up with footy, it was in your blood.'

The experience of football grounds, football players and the thrill of a game infected Kirsten, As a child, she used to jump the barriers when the hooter sounded the end of a game, so she could run and touch the backs of her favourite players.

'Alex Jesaulenko was my hero, but he was so tall I couldn't reach his back, I touched his knee once.

'We'd follow the players to the change room and I was stopped from going inside while all the little boys were allowed to, and that was a really pivotal moment in my political development. I was mortified. I went away and wondered what was so strange and sacred in there that my brothers could go in but I couldn't.

'Rather than being filled with resentment, I decided that one day I was going to find out what was going on in there, and I have! 'Coaching is not as daunting as a lot of people imagine. The players are the least of your worries, they are far too selfish to worry about whether they are being coached by a man or a woman. All they want to do is play, play well and win. If you can help them get there you'll have the same respect as any other coach.

'If I had this chance years ago, I would have been tempted to make football my career.'

Early in the '90s the Sydney Football League hosted a game which was umpired solely by all women. Kirsten feels that women won't just continue to make a mark in coaching circles, but honestly believes that we will see female players at the top level in our lifetime.

'There are women who are as tall, as strong and as fast as a lot of men who play. The woman who breaks through would have to be exceptional but one day someone will stop having the doors slammed in her face, and just go in and do it.'

Now for some honesty – what is it that Kirsten really likes about the job?

'I must admit, there is an element of self restraint in the job – it's like letting a kid loose in a candy store. I'm surrounded by gorgeous young men.

'I remember one of the things that first hit me when I moved to Sydney, and saw a crowd shot of the rugby league, I kept thinking there was something wrong with it. Finally I looked at a closeup of an AFL crowd and it dawned on me – there weren't nearly enough women in the rugby league crowds. My philosophy is that the men's bodies in AFL are much more attractive and that's why women make up a greater portion of the crowd in Aussie Rules.

'But now I've got the ultimate job. I don't only get the chance to eye off some great players, I also get to boss them around!'

One thing that constantly amazes me is that while women are keen to learn and support men's sport, there isn't that much eagerness from men to support the women's side of sport. Given that nearly half the crowds at some footy games now are women, you'd think that we'd demand that the girl's teams be given ago. But we don't do we? Why not?

Girls, I think if we're going to be serious about this footy stuff, we should be just as serious with the women's teams. Give them a go. If you get a chance to join a club, do it. If you can't play, get involved in setting up the games or looking after the drinks, or even just turning up to support them. You'd probably learn about the game more quickly than if you tried to jump straight into the professional world of men. Give it some thought.

THE MEDIA

MEDIA

THE MEDIA

HOW TO FOLLOW THE MEDIA

If you read everything written, listened to everything broadcast and watched everything televised on footy, you would need your week to be about 17 days long.

It is not humanly possible to absorb all the information there is about footy – whichever code – and still there are people out there who want more!

There are footy shows on TV all year. Through the winter live footy broadcasts dominate AM radio and every day you can find footy news in the papers.

Then there are the specialist media – there are football programs to buy at all the games, there are weekly footy magazines, monthly footy magazines and quarterly publications as well as the annuals. There are newsletters if you belong to a specific club, and even weekly videos if you're too lazy to read and would prefer to watch the weekend highlights.

The beauty about accessing non-stop football info is that you need never feel that you've missed out. It goes on and on and on.

I have a friend who confines herself to her bedroom all weekend, every weekend, so she doesn't miss out on any footy action. She has five television sets in her room and four radio sets. She tunes into one TV station on Saturdays for their league coverage, another on Friday and Sunday nights for the other league games, a separate station again for the AFL, SBS for soccer and Channel 10 for Sports Tonight, which provides a full wrap of all codes. Living in Sydney she has three radio sets tuned into the AM stations which provide a full coverage of a variety of rugby league games and rugby union news. The fourth set is tuned into NewsRadio for their AFL coverage.

Going home from work on Fridays she stops at the newsagent to buy *Sports Weekly*, *Inside Sport*, *Rugby League Week*, *Soccer Weekly*, *Rugby Union Week* and the AFL rag. She orders pizza, stocks up on Coke and settles down for a wonderful weekend.

I've heard so many other girls say, 'Why doesn't she get a life?'. The answer is, 'She's got one!'. Come Monday mornings she's got more guys talking to her than the rest of the building put together. She can tell you who won, who was injured, who was sent off, how badly the refs or umpires performed, what the ladder looks like and who's going to have to face the judiciary later in the week.

You might not be able to dedicate yourself to such a degree, and there are some shortcuts. However, like any other kind of fitness, footy-fitness requires just a little bit of work every day.

Let's create a schedule that is personally designed for your very own needs. From the suggestions that follow, pick the components that best suit your lifestyle and football needs:

MONDAY

Step 1

Get into the habit of listening to the early morning news bulletins on AM radio so that you get a complete review of the weekend footy action before you get to school or work. You will be an instant hit with your cab driver on the way to work, with the people sitting next to you on the bus, train, or tram, and with your colleagues if you can remember just two or three key things from the news, such as:

1. Who's gone to the top of the ladder

2. Who's gone to the bottom of the ladder

3. Who will face the judiciary

Those three vital pieces of information can lead to a good four or five hour chat that can be spread throughout your day.

If you have a difficult boss or a school teacher you don't seem to be able to get on with, find out which footy team they support. On Monday morning as you walk by, quietly mutter 'Fantastic win by the Dogs yesterday!'. It is sure to earn you a whole lot more respect. One of the greatest aspects of footy is that it unites people who would otherwise have nothing in common.

To get into the habit of catching an early Monday morning footy wrap, it's best to set your radio alarm to the local footy station. Pretty soon your whole household will become accustomed to the 6am footy-news each Monday.

Step 2

On your way to school or work (after listening to the radio news), back up the info you've already got with a bit more in-depth analysis. This is where the daily newspapers come into their own.

Every paper, except the Financial Review, will carry a detailed footy section, allowing you to find out the specifics of any particular game that interests you. Flick first to the scores and results and have a look at that footy ladder. Take a mental picture of it so that when you overhear somebody asking where Geelong are on the ladder you'll be able to respond almost immediately, 'Fourth place after their win on the weekend'. It's so easy to sound like a genius!

Newspaper coverage of footy, or any sport, is terrific. It's full of animation, energy and emotion. Stories often recall sensational moments in a game – moments that will become history, situations that will forever change the way footy is played and therefore change the fabric of Australian culture.

Recite a couple of these passages of play so that when somebody asks you about the highlight of your weekend you can say, 'When Smithy scooped up the ball like a shovelful of sand and swept it up towards his shoulder before charging down the fearsome opposition and dodging the calculating fullback to dive into the corner post and put the ball down like he was setting a diamond into a wedding ring. That try was the most wonderful moment of my weekend.' You'll have every dedicated footyhead around you weeping over that glorious moment.

Newspapers will also highlight all of the controversies from the weekend games and predict alternative outcomes. Once you've tired of reliving moments from the weekend you can move on to talk about why Conners will front the judiciary tonight and only be given a two week suspension instead of a six week holiday as some others are suggesting. You will find all the arguments you need in the newspaper reports.

Note well: NEVER, EVER, EVER read a newspaper any other way except back to front. If you read the front pages before turning to the back, where the sports pages are generally located, you will give yourself away as a pretender. You MUST start with the sports news. Everything else is gloss, really.

Step 3

After a tough start to the week, come home, kick back and put on the telly. Forget the news – you can talk right over the top of all that stuff about elections and strikes and discrimination cases. But the minute you hear the word 'Sportswrap', make sure everybody in the house moves into the cone of silence. This is important. This is earth-shattering news; NOT to be missed.

Listen for updates on injuries, possible team changes for next

SOCCER COMMENTATOR: ANDY PASCALIDES

Andy started commentating soccer on radio and television back in 1984 but all the way through school as a soccer-crazed kid he used to call 'pretend' matches into his tape recorder. (You thought footy players were obsessive – footy commentators are MAD!)

He discovered soccer one Saturday when he was walking to Greek school and saw the local team practising on the field. Needless to say, he skipped Greek school that day, and all the Saturdays that followed, to sit and watch his new found heroes.

Andy admits to being aware of the 'first-time listener' while he's calling games and says that's why he prefers an emotional call as opposed to a technically correct one.

'The temptation is to direct your commentary towards fanatical soccer experts, because it's almost like a competition – who knows more about the game.

'But you have to be realistic...you have to include some of the basics for the first-time listeners, because if you can generalise more, you become more informative and entertaining for them.'

In the early days of live sports commentary, everything was extremely correct and there was hardly any emotion. That's changing these days, because sports commentators realise that if they want you to listen they must be entertaining.

'I'm an emotional commentator; I prefer the passion of the game and I thrive on the crowd's emotion. If you can relay that to an audience, you're doing a good job.

'That's why I prefer radio commentary to television commentary. The words tell the picture on radio and the listener gets to use his or her imagination – you shut everything else out and become obsessed. It's just a great feeling.

'My advice for first-timers is to tune into a game you have something in common with, like a player or a team that you follow, and sit down with your radio and let it absorb you. You'll be hooked.'

weekend and the very latest on judicial hearings. This will put you in the right frame of mind to pop into bed and dream footy all night long. You will find that you'll start waking up fresher and fresher each morning as you become footy-fit because even one football dream a night makes you wake feeling refreshed and ready to tackle the world again! Sweet dreams.

TUESDAY

Step 1

If you don't feel that you can take the pressure of a seven day a week footy-fit campaign, then Tuesday should be your day off.

It's a good idea to still have your alarm set to the footy station of your choice so that you can catch the latest on the tribunal hearings but other than that...hey, think of more mundane things to give your mind a rest – the mortgage, the kids, the homework, the amount you owe on your credit card and simple things of that nature. Believe me, only one day off football and on to thinking about all the other problems in life, and you'll be keen to get straight back into your footy-fit campaign tomorrow.

WEDNESDAY

Step 1

Radio news. By now, last weekend's games are history and all the focus is on next weekend. Sure, they are still four or five days away, but it's good to be prepared. It's time to start specu-lating over who's going to be put in or taken out of the team, about how the weather will affect the ground for Saturday's match and about whether the coach will keep his job if the team loses again.

If you have some extra time, spend a little bit listening to the radio, because you're likely to hear some intelligent talkback conversation somewhere on the dial that will really challenge your thinking. Usually someone will interview a player later in the afternoon. Have your wits about you. You think following the Dow Jones is difficult? Try interpreting what your average footballer is on about! If you can make sense of the interview you're a mile ahead of the opposition, and that puts you in a very commanding position. You can actually become his translator.

Because relatively few other people would have understood what was said, you can transcribe it and sound as if you actually know the bloke. Act as though it was something he told you on the phone earlier on! This is fantastic...football can be a fantasy come true!

Step 2

Newspaper time. Same deal. Buy your favourite rag from the newsagent, but also keep your eyes open today for the proper footy magazine. It should be hitting the stands soon and the bonus of getting a proper footy mag as opposed to the regular paper is that footy mags are written the way footy players would talk. There are a couple of words missing here and there and some of the descriptions are a little bit hazy, but it helps you to think the way a footy player would, and that makes you more game-perceptive. When your favourite player makes an interesting decision on the footy field next weekend, you'll be able to relate to it, because you read his interview in the footy magazine earlier in the week and understand the way his brain works.

There are also photos! And centrefolds! And autographs, competitions, quotes, cross-words, all sorts of great footy things to keep you entertained.

Step 3

Watch the TV news on your favourite channel and, depending on which state of Australia you live in and which code of football you follow, you might be able to tune into one of the footy shows tonight. They are a bag of laughs. All the stars come on, they talk about nothing except footy, they show a few highlights and they predict how the rest of the season will go. Footy shows are a must.

Some friends of mine play a game while watching footy shows. If you feel you've heard it all before when you're watching the

300th footy player get interviewed, turn the volume down and try to lip-read. Lip-reading a footy player is like trying to read Braille with gardening gloves on. It's a hell of a lot of fun but you probably won't be successful. Of course, not too many footballers have won awards for diction and pronunciation, but you'll catch on.

Interestingly, if you do play this little 'guess what I'm saying' game, you will find out that players from each club have specific little characteristics. For example, everyone from Carlton uses words three or four syllables long, whereas if they're from the Crows their fringes are longer than their sentences. In rugby league, coastal teams will say everything is 'fully':

'Training was fully hard.'
'It was fully rigged.'
'Tonkers was fully aggro about that one.'

While inland teams might describe all things as 'awesome':

'The ground looks awesome today.'
'It was an awesome feeling scoring that try.'
'Awesome crowd last night, awesome.'

After a fun night of lip-reading your favourite footy player, you will enjoy another great night in bed.

THURSDAY

Step 1
Radio, of course. You'll need to concentrate pretty hard today because it's getting towards the 'business end of the week' – this is a cliche you'll probably hear all day today and tomorrow. Keep your ears open for news on injuries that might have occurred at training and the odd slinging match which normally gets underway between rival teams about this time each week.

Because there's not a hell of a lot else to talk about, most of the quotes will be talking about this weekend's opponents. Some of the stuff you're likely to hear may include:

'We trashed them last time we played, and we expect more of the same this weekend.'
'Yeah, we lost to them last time we played, but they've been like a pack of donkeys on the field recently. We'll run all over them.'

If you listen to footy-talk regularly, you'll be able to start guessing which of the politicians follow football. Pollies nearly all start to copy their favourite footballer and sooner or later they start yelling out their favourite quotes in parliament. It's obvious that both Paul Keating and John Howard have been long-time football supporters: listening to some of their lines, you'd think they were moonlighting as footy coaches.

Step 2

The papers. More predictions, a word or two from the coaches and more veiled threats about what to expect on the weekend. Some analysis from the reporters will give you all the scoops you need to get you through another tough day.

Step 3

TV. There will be footy news galore on television tonight as all channels try to grab your attention so that you stay there from now till the weekend and help boost their ratings points so that they can charge advertisers more money to advertise on their channel.

Tonight is the night for seeing a bit of training action. Most stations will venture out to training and get some shots of players pretending to sprint, tackling punching bags and kicking balls up and down the field. This provides a rare opportunity to see what

RUGBY UNION COMMENTATOR: GORDON BRAY

'I started off as a trainee with ABC Sport. In my spare time I'd go to the Sydney Sports Ground and call rugby league matches into my tape recorder for practice. I did that for two years, I was so keen to call football.

'I was transferred to Hobart and the first game I got to call on air was an Aussie Rules match. It was a game between New Norfolk and North Hobart and I'll never forget it because the sports editor introduced me as a rugby commentator from Sydney, so my credibility went straight out the window.

'I've called all the football codes. When I'm commentating I try to visualise a few people watching the game on TV in their loungeroom. I try to talk to them, rather than at them. It would be wrong to direct commentary to a particular group – say males over 30 – I try to keep it simple enough for an average family: mum, dad and the two kids. I have a 7-year-old daughter and I try to keep her in mind in case she's watching.

'There are basic principles that apply to radio and television commentary – you need to identify, enthuse, anticipate as well as entertain and provide background information. Radio requires more colourful and continuous commentary whereas TV gives you time to pause as you let the pictures tell the story.

'What I've learnt is that you can't please everybody any time, and it would be a miracle if you pleased anybody all the time.

'If people are looking at getting involved in football for the first time, I'd suggest soccer – it's got good skills and is easy to understand. Also, on TV, rugby league translates well – a game on TV is often far more exciting than watching it live because of the close ups on the hit-ups which you see from every angle. AFL's religious zeal, as far as supporters go, is exciting, and rugby union needs to simplify the laws and the coaches need to become far more positive in their approach. They need to have a view towards entertainment and enjoyment for themselves and the spectators because that's what sport is all about.

'As far as women's football goes, I've refereed plenty of matches and there aren't too many differences. When they change their tops at half-time it's different and the language is worse – especially in their pep talks. But they're a lot of fun to referee because good women's teams now are very skilled and their ball retention is excellent. There are women's teams in Canberra, Sydney and Brisbane that are better than some of the men's teams playing grade competition.'

footballers look like outside their footy uniforms. Some of them train in tracksuits, others in cycle shorts and some in surf gear. Seeing your favourite player in something other than his weekend uniform makes him look so much more vulnerable. All of a sudden he turns from a gladiator into a real man.

FRIDAY

Step 1

Radio. Pre-weekend nerves are wound right up and there should be some newsworthy footy information to report this morning. This is the ideal time to pick up the weekend weather forecast and catch all the experts' predictions so that you can place a bet at the TAB later in the day.

You will find, as you become more accustomed to the various commentators on each of the stations, that you will start to select a couple of favourites – ones whose ideas you like and agree with. Be selective in your choices, and when it comes down to a tough 'tipping' selection, go with the commentator you like best.

By evening time a Friday night match might be broadcast on your local footy station, which is great news! If you're going out you can listen to it in the car on the way, and during the evening you can discreetly wear an earplug connected to the Walkman in your handbag, or if you're at home, you can turn on the radio coverage while watching the TV!

It's a common habit for sports fans to turn the volume on their TV sets down to zero while listening to the commentary on radio. There are two basic reasons. Radio has fewer ad breaks (and if it's the ABC there are no ad breaks) and the commentary itself is different. Listen for yourself. Because radio commentators don't have the advantage of pictures to tell their story, they need to use

RUGBY LEAGUE COMMENTATOR: PETER WILKINS

'Wilko' started calling soccer for the ABC in 1981 at the World Youth Championships and still remembers his first game: Australia versus Cameroon.

'I was sitting out in the crowd and was really self-conscious about the people around me listening to what I thought was a very average call – it's the quickest way to learn.'

After eight years of calling soccer for radio and TV Wilko moved on to rugby league commentary in 1989. He says this is much easier to call because it's a much more ordered game and therefore easier for the audience to follow as well.

'In league you have set plays, scrums and a fairly formatted game overall. Soccer is less ordered and you have to keep identifying players, as well as keeping up with the ball which sometimes moves between seven pairs of feet within about three seconds!'

Wilko agrees with Andy that commentators of the '90s should use their emotion to get the story across and that a combination of TV pictures and radio sound is the best way to learn.

'It's only fair that the commentator gives a bit of his emotion, because the players are out there giving all of theirs and the commentator has to relay everything that's happening on the field to the audience.

'Having the TV on with the radio volume up is the best way to catch on to a game, no matter what the code, because you see it all and have the frenetic commentary explaining everything.

'As a commentator, I have to assume that everybody has a reasonable level of understanding of the game, otherwise they wouldn't be listening, but if you're trying to learn, there should still be enough pieces for you to pick up to start putting the jigsaw puzzle together.'

words to build the pictures. It means their commentary is far more colourful and descriptive than most TV commentary.

Step 2

Papers. Friday is a 'must' day for papers. You will generally find the draw for weekend games, team lists, comparisons of teams and all the background information necessary. Often it's all written up in a liftout, so that once you've bought the whole paper, you can actually just lift out the sports section and chuck the rest away.

Step 3

TV. Plenty on tonight – footy programs, sports shows, even a televised game or two! This is how you know the weekend has really started. You get a couple of bottles of your favourite fizzy drink on the way home, buy a frozen food pack to heat up in the microwave and settle down on the beanbag with a couple of your best mates to watch the footy! You will find yourself in heaven.

The commentators come on and tell you how exciting it is to be at 'this great game'. They give their predictions, have a little argument or two between themselves and then the ref blows the whistle or bounces the ball to start the match. Now is the time to get jumpy. Your adrenalin will start pumping as if it was you out there on the footy field running around in the mud and rain and freezing conditions and having the time of your life!

If you are REALLY new at the game, don't say too much while you're watching the broadcast – just listen. The commentators have been following the game for years and most of them are former players of some degree so their experience shines through. What you have to do is work on synchronising their comments with moves that you see on the ground. Slow motion replays are really handy here.

Watch the slow motion replays really carefully and listen to what the commentators say so that when the game resumes you know what to look for. Once you pick up a couple of tactics players use, you'll soon be able to point them out quicker than the commentators. Your footyhead friends will be REALLY impressed.

You'll notice that particular players have their own little habits – you can use these to identify them from the pack. Australian Wallaby George Gregan has a habit of tucking his shirt in while he's running with the ball to score a try. Kangaroo Rod Wishart does a little war dance before coming in to strike the ball at goal. Watch for these repetitive moves and learn to recognise the players from them.

At halftime and fulltime in the TV coverage some analysis will be given by the experts. Don't tune out. These times are vital. This is your homework time. It may not be a whole lot of fun, but 20 minutes or so of listening to the wrap-up is like cramming for an exam – it CAN work.

In only a couple of weeks you will start to see the game much more clearly. You may even find yourself disagreeing with the commentators. That's when you know you've made the grade – you can see things that the experts couldn't. Give yourself a clap.

SATURDAY

Step 1

You should wake up feeling really good this morning. You've experienced a game overnight, probably dreamt about all your favourite players, and now you've woken up knowing it will all happen again this afternoon!

Radio today is full of footy. Tune in and have a listen to the summaries from last night's games, and listen to the talkback callers and see if you agree with them. If you don't, call in yourself and let them know what you think!

Can you imagine what sort of reaction you'll get from all the footyheads at school or the office next week when you arrive and they've heard you on talkback radio over the weekend? You'll be surprised at just how many people (and who!) listen to sports radio. Give it a go – test it out!

The beauty of radio is that it is so immediate. If news breaks, it'll be on the airwaves NOW.

AUSSIE RULES COMMENTATOR: TIM LANE

Unlike the other commentators, Tim Lane doesn't think of any particular audience while he's broadcasting – unless he's aware of somebody in particular that is tuned in on a special day which can add a degree of importance to your call.

'It can be a bit daunting if you think about who's listening – especially with football, because everyone will listen at some stage!

'I remember Brian Johnston (one of the world's most famous cricket commentators from the BBC) telling how he was instructed to imagine he was broadcasting to blind people. There are various other anecdotes, but they don't work for me. I just try to do it. If something good happens, it happens naturally. But there are other commentators who have a much better capacity for theatrics, and they can plan certain aspects of a call which will come off. I think a genuine love of the game,

caring for the game and being excited by it will affect what comes out of a commentator's mouth.'

Tim's love affair with football began with his first game.

'I was living in Tasmania. My dad took me to my first game when I was four. It had an immediate impact. It was real life theatre. There was a sense of my team representing all that was good, while any other team was the image of darkness and evil.

'Football is a competitive, dramatic performance without a script nobody knows what will happen not even the players who are acting out the drama. Added to that there is the colour of it all, and the crowd.

'When you're little even 1,000 people can look like a huge crowd and the only other place a kid sees such a large audience is probably at church! The whole thing really excited me.'

If you find yourself rushing off to a barbie at one of your friends' houses, or at the local park, and you know there will be a couple of armchair footy experts attending, just tune in to a radio sportshow for ten minutes or so on your way there and you will be armed with all the information you'll need for the afternoon!

While there will be hours of chat and interviews on radio early in the day, once the games kick off, between 2 and 3pm you can catch all the live descriptions. Don't worry if there's no TV handy – you can access all the games on radio. The bonus with radio

TIM LANE CONTINUED

The question is often asked, 'Why don't women call football?' There's a huge perception out there that more women would listen to or watch football coverage if a woman was part of the commentary team. Despite the fact that very few women, if any, apply for commentary positions when they are advertised, Tim believes the issue goes much deeper than that.

'There is a traditional divide that women have to cross. It hasn't happened yet, which raises the question, 'Will it ever happen?' I think it could but I have no idea when. There's a perception that because I'm male I've played the game, so my sex immediately adds authority and experience to a broadcast. That may, or may not be the case, but that's the psychology behind it. Because it's not women on the field, there's an underlying perception that they couldn't relate as well as men. Even though women play the game, there are a lot of other women that don't take them seriously.

'If you consider the origins of contact sport, it's very gladiatorial. The football codes are very much a physical battle with the concept of standing together and fighting hard. It's possible football will always remain the domain of men, especially with aspects like tackling which is centred around the chest. I don't know what it would be like for a woman to be tackled strongly around the chest area but I imagine it would be pretty painful. Today, especially, we're educated to the importance of protecting women's breasts.

'Commentary tends to reflect what's happening on the field. It has a male nature. Nevertheless, if a woman came along with the same passion, desire and ability, and felt comfortable in the environment, I'm sure doors would open for her.'

coverage is that while the station you choose may focus on one particular game, they constantly go 'around the grounds' – scores from all other matches are updated about every five minutes.

Step 2

The newspapers will be full of descriptive stories about last night's game. Read some of them and see if you agree. There will also be updates on injuries and reports for bad behaviour – these will be key discussion points in any group you are part of over the weekend. Also look at the analytical stories that describe how last night's results really do affect society and mankind. You can never overplay the importance of a footy result. For example:

Carlton's win over Geelong last night means that Footscray's last-ditch attempt against the Crows is a crucial one.

Interpretation: Every game is bloody important.

Step 3

Time to turn that television set back on! It's time for the double-header! In some states you can get two games broadcast on the one afternoon. This is known as 'Lazy Saturday' – you won't even be able to get out of the house. Just sit yourself down with a tinny and some chips and bask in the glory of footy all day long!

Most Saturdays there'll only be one game televised, though, and while early on you might think 'thank goodness for that', believe me, the more involved you get in football, the more you will hang out for the lazy Saturdays.

SUNDAY

Step 1

By now you should be aching. You should feel as though you've played all the games so far this weekend. You might have a bit of a headache from all the information that's been pumped in, your hammies (hamstrings) might feel tender and you may even have a groin strain. That is all part of being a footyhead. As time progresses you'll start to enjoy the pain.

Roll out of bed slowly and put the radio on to catch the latest news.

Step 2

Run outside and buy the Sunday papers, then lounge around for a while reading all the scandal. Sunday papers generally have more room, and the journalists have had all week to write their stories, so they can be much juicier and contain a bit of gossip.

For those who prefer photos, there're more of those in the Sunday papers too. Check out those muscles, look at the speed, stare into the eyes of your favourite footballer. It's a nice way to start the day. If your boyfriend, or husband, questions you on the fact that you've been looking at one page for three hours just tell him you're not looking at the sexy photos, you're reading the interesting articles. He'll know all about that.

Step 3

Yes, there'll be more football on TV. You will almost be numbed by it all come Sunday afternoon, so perhaps this is the day you should make the effort to GO to the game.

This is a whole new life experience.

Select your outfit carefully depending on which part of the ground you are going to sit in and plan accordingly. Do you need to take an esky with your own drinks? Do you need to take your own food or will the cold meat pies and soggy chips do? How many raincoats, umbrellas, jumpers should you take? Will you make up a banner to wave as your favourite player runs by? Decisions, decisions – it's so much fun.

Don't forget – if you're going to the game on a Sunday you'll probably find yourself caught up in the tide heading back to the club afterwards. Make sure you have something warm and clean to put on as well as a little dash of perfume to hide that sweat you might have worked up during the game! (I know it's not a nice topic to talk about, but it's better to be prepared than to ignore what could be an embarrassing situation!)

Step 4

You should be about ready to collapse. You've had a terrific weekend and what you've learnt about footy in just seven days is remarkable.

You deserve an award. But remember, it all starts again tomorrow morning. Mondays are extremely important because that's when you get the chance to boast about your own real life experiences when you get to school or work. Be prepared. You're playing your own game here, and just as you like to see your own footy team win, it's also a great feeling to win the Monday morning argument over which team played best, worst and fairest, and which player deserved the man of the match award. The more informed you are, the better your footy arguing will be.

TV PRODUCER: GERRY O'LEARY

Women today are making a strong move into the very male – dominated roles of sports production and administration. One of the movers and shakers is Gerry O'Leary, ABC TV's supervisor of sports production.

Back in 1985 Gerry was employed as a producer's assistant to learn all about TV's coverage of rugby league. She never felt out of place because she was confident in her knowledge of the sport after growing up with three brothers who were always kicking a footy around the back yard.

'Football was a real way of life for me from a very early age - I had my first cigarette at a footy game and my first kiss. Footy has some great memories for me and it's ironic that now I earn my living from the game.'

In somewhat of a role reversal, Gerry had to teach her husband about the wonders of the game after he started questioning her astonishing habit of cementing herself in front of the television set every time a match was being broadcast.

'My husband's a drama teacher and he had no interest in footy at all. He was just mystified about my enthusiasm and love of the sport.'

'When State of Origin rolled around he could see my energy and interest and he stopped and said, "Well, there must be something good in all of this", so he gave it a go.

'He knows all the players now and what's going on, so we can actually share in the enjoyment of it all.'

In the early '90s the rugby league producer's role became available and Gerry snapped it up. Producing and directing the ABC's coverage involves deciding on camera positions, looking at lighting in commentary boxes, liaising with players, working out halftime entertainment, directing the cameras during the coverage, coming up with the program ideas for either side of the game and making the editorial decisions.

'It was funny when I first started dealing with the NSW Rugby League and the various teams. I'd make appointments with people and they'd all be shocked when I turned up because my name's Gerry, and they always expected a man.'

As far as getting involved in football:

'It's so easy – you can learn about the game by reading the papers and just exposing yourself to the media coverage. Once you go to a game the spark will turn into a fire and you'll be hooked.

'You might originally think, 'Oh my God, go to the footy', but get your man or your friends to take you and sit there and absorb the atmosphere and get into it...you are allowed to cheer and roar and enjoy yourself. It's fun to scream your head off; it's an opportunity to release your emotions. There's nothing like being at the footy enjoying a meat pie and Coke.'

KATE PATON, CHANNEL 7 SPORTS REPORTER

'Aussie Rules is the staple diet of any Victorian and I'm an ardent Hawthorn supporter!

'I grew up with lots of male cousins and was brought up on the exploits of a couple of AFL legends – 'Jezza' (Alex Jesaulenko) and 'The Mighty Blues' (Carlton) – but was forced to change allegiances during the mid '80s when one of my cousins, Chris Langford, started playing for the Hawks.

'Having the men race in to commandeer the television set when footy coverage began never worried me - to be honest, I beat them to it! Because I work weekends I actually see less sport now than I used to, but I manage to get to quite a few games during the season, and I watch at least one game and two replays a weekend. I'll go to most of the finals and haven't missed seeing a Grand Final since I was 13.

'The best way to learn is to go on the hunt for somebody sympathetic who will explain the rules to you and it's easiest if you only watch the top teams until you get the hang of it. Any sport at its best is engaging.

'One of the greatest joys for me is playing kick-to-kick in the office with the likes of former greats Bob Davis or Neil Kerley – there is nothing quite like booting the perfect (or as close as possible) torpedo in such company – and I'd recommend giving it a go to anyone on whom the finer points of the game are lost. Once you've tried it, you'll start to understand. Promise!'

JOHANNA SWEET, CHANNEL 7 SPORTS PRESENTER

'I follow all codes of football, but my favourites are rugby league and aussie rules. In the league I follow my local team, Manly, and have done so for as long as I can remember. In the aussie rules I follow the Sydney Swans.

'I try to get to as many games as I can for both the aussie rules and the league – if I'm working on weekends, which is usually the case, I have the TV monitors in our office switched on to both codes! I always try to attend the Grand Final and if I do get the odd weekend off, my husband Gary and I head to his home town of Adelaide or to Melbourne and make sure we get out to watch whoever is playing.

'I have memories of collecting wheelbarrows full of maroon and white flowers with my brother and sisters and showering all the passing cars with Manly colours – especially when Manly was winning Grand Final after Grand Final. As for the aussie rules, my husband played for 17 years and has always been a mad Collingwood and Crows supporter and my grandfather played representative football for years. So I guess there is a solid base for an interest in the code, yet it wasn't till I started work with Channel 7 that I really learnt to love the game. I had to present the halftime segment each weekend, giving out the local results and profiling players. I now work closely with the Sydney Swans and the NSW and Australian Football Leagues and love every minute of it.

'To get involved, I'd suggest going to a match of whatever code takes your fancy with somebody who loves it and can explain it to you. I find that the majority of complaints I hear about football are from people who don't actually know what's going on. It's amazing the difference a clear understanding of the rules and strategies can make to your enjoyment of the game!'

KATHRYN LAMOND, CHANNEL 10 SPORTS REPORTER

'Rugby league is my game, but as a kid I used to watch the soccer. I'd sit up late at night with my dad and watch the FA Cup, so I started learning about the game that way. My first real boyfriend was a soccer player.

'The game you follow all depends upon proximity and what's played close to home. I know there was always a rugby league game being played out in the street by all the kids and I actually chipped a front tooth making a really good tackle on one of the boys when I was pretty little!

'Because of my job I follow all the codes, really. The best way to learn is to start recognising a few of the personalities, then follow their team and all the ups and downs on a regular basis. Map your team and see how they go. By the time the finals roll around, you'll be so intoxicated that you just can't help getting caught up in it all.

'If you really don't like footy to begin with, it can be hard and tedious trying to learn, but forget the rule book – that's too much like studying for an exam. You won't enjoy it. As I said, learn about the personalities first and the rest will follow.

'Once you start identifying with the players, then you can look at skill and speed and start to follow the tussle between the adversaries to see who'll win the battle. It really isn't as hard and complicated as the guys make out. Look at the big picture, then slowly break it down and you'll learn to recognise the basic mistakes and before you know it you'll be talking footy on the same level as all the guys you know.'

SPORTS MEDIA HAS ITS MOMENTS

Working in the sports media sometimes has it's moments too: 'KING WALLY' is not a character out of a fairy tale. He is a real life footy legend who has become the unofficial monarch of Queensland.

Wally Lewis is one of those players who couldn't describe what he actually did on a footy field because it wasn't learned, it was all instinctive. Sure, he worked hard and trained hard but he was one of the few chosen ones born with an incredible athletic ability. He read a game like he was reading a nursery rhyme. It was all so simple.

Wally was part of a successful Australian Schoolboy's Rugby Union tour in 1977–78 before switching to the professional code of rugby league. He became captain of Australia and captain of Queensland for the very successful State of Origin concept which was born in 1980. He became the world's best five eighth and made the No.6 Maroon Jumper worth a fortune.

After retiring from the game in 1992 he became coach of Queensland, which had dominated the interstate series throughout his playing days. Unfortunately he didn't enjoy the same success as coach.

During the 1994 campaign, King Wally's Queenslanders were beaten by NSW. Aside from his reputation as a genius player, Wally had also earned a reputation as a shocking loser – a common symptom for champion sportspeople.

I happened to be at the last game of the 1994 State of Origin series and once the whistle had been blown it was one of the commentators' jobs to go down to the dressing rooms and interview both the winning and losing coaches. All five men working on the coverage that night volunteered to interview Phil Gould, the winning NSW coach. Not suprisingly, there weren't many hands put up to interview the King.

What was surprising was that a tape recorder and microphone were thrown into my lap and I was told to go interview Wally. 'Well, that's funny,' I thought, 'I'm on a night off – I'm not even working . . . these blokes have all whimped out and I've ended up with one of the most daunting tasks a sports commentator can have: interviewing the King after a loss!'

I went down to the Queensland dressing rooms with my heart beating solidly in my throat. I knocked on the door only faintly, hoping nobody would hear me and I could escape. Unfortunately a rotund little man opened the door slightly and asked what I wanted.

'I'm from the ABC, here to interview Wally Lewis.'

'Good luck!' the official laughed. Great. That filled me with confidence.

He led me into the inner sanctum of the Queensland dressing rooms. All the players had showered and were drowning their sorrows elsewhere but Wally was left, teary eyed, head hanging, one foot up on a bench, arms leaning on his leg as he fiddled with a lead pencil. My heart bled for him. This was no way for a King to be seen by one of his people.

'Excuse me Wally, Tracey Holmes from ABC Radio, I'd like to ask you a couple of questions please.'

I never imagined such a simple question would evoke such a dramatic reply.

The lead pencil was now a collection of splinters as Wally snapped it a thousand times before hurling it past my head and into the far dressing room wall. The three officials that had been trying to console him disolved into the cement floor and completely disappeared, leaving me alone with one angry king.

'If you (expletive) think I'm going to (expletive) answer any (expletive) questions you've got another (expletive) thing coming!' the King bellowed.

Having never experienced anything quite so frightening I didn't know what to do, so like all nervous sports commentators do in a moment of pressure I pressed the record button on my tape recorder and held the microphone to Wally's lips.

Without a hitch, he continued, showing what a true professional he was 'Yes, I'm extremely disappointed not just for me but for the guys too – State of Origin is so special, it means so much...'

Wally Lewis is a former winner of the 'Golden Boot' award for the greatest player in the world. I'd like to present him with 'The Golden Microphone Award' for being as professional off the field as he was on it.

TTING

TIPPING

SIDELIGHT OR DISTRACTION

At the MCG, Carlton have thrashed Geelong to win the 1995 Grand Final. You knew it was going to happen that way, didn't you? You were tempted to back that judgement with some hard-earned pocket money, but didn't quite know how, or were a tad embarrassed about the thought of placing a bet. I mean, what would everyone think?

Settle down. Betting and tipping is as much a part of football folklore as the game itself. There are strategies, benefits and pitfalls. (I hope I'll be able to alert you to some of those). Of course, you may already be a self-made millionaire from footy punting – if you are, give me a call!

The first thing you need to recognise about gambling on the footy is that it can be an entertaining sideline or a total distraction – there are so many options at your disposal. With the right organisation, be it the local TAB or betting shop, or agencies such as Centrebet, you can have a flutter on anything: who will score the first try in a game, who will kick the first goal, the highest-scoring game of the round, the score of a game, the margin of victory, who's going to leave the field injured first! That last one may be a bit fanciful, but in the true Aussie tradition, you can bet on anything. All you need is your own inclination to place a bet and someone to accept the wager.

HOW TO ANALYSE FORM

If you've ever been to a race track for a day of champagne and galloping, you'll know that many of your best selections have been made by that age-old method of blind finger pointing or on the strength of a name and how sweet it sounds. Sometimes, on the other hand, you've lamented your lack of preparation. Oh, what a touch more homework might have done to your finances!

Footy punting is no different. Often you will just have that gut feeling about a winner, a first scorer, or a margin, and it could prove successful. However, there's no question that some studious work on the form can increase your chances of victory.

Which team to back

One of the oldest theories about tipping or gambling on the result of a match is the history of results between the two sides. Players or long-term supporters in any code will tell you with absolute assurance that the weekend opponent is the bogey team. Your team might have it all over this bogey opponent in terms of current form and position on the table, but upstairs, in the mind-game zone, the doubts persist: 'Gee, we've never beaten this mob on their home ground', or 'I just hate this ground, it doesn't feel right'.

It's extremely important when assessing the form for the weekend tipping competition, or a dabble on one game in particular, to know the background of results between the teams. This is easily found. The newspaper previews usually mention it somewhere, and the weekly footy magazine of your choosing will have all the vital statistics.

Once you've organised that side of the equation, it's time to get down to the serious business of 'recent form'. How many points or goals has your team been registering? What about the style of their victories over the last few weeks? Are they on a roll, or is the form a little more spasmodic? Think about the ground conditions - weather forecasts for the day, how the team performs in the wet or dry. Who's in or out for the day on both sides and who's refereeing or umpiring (more on this in a moment)! Already you're three parts of the way to success. Most importantly though, remember not to ignore that spur-of-the-moment thought or feeling in the pit of the stomach - these can be just as important as the factual data gleaned through your extensive homework.

I'll let you in on a secret: I go with gut feeling first, current position on the ladder second and calibre of the opponent third. Last year I finished middle of the road in the tipping contest, which is nothing to be proud of I know, but the year before I was beaten by a point in the final round by somebody who should have been drug tested! But, hey, no hard feelings. The lesson is – luck will always play a part – well 50% luck and 50% homework. The most important ingredient is fun – you've got to enjoy doing it. It's amazing how many positive people have all the luck! he real down-and-out, gloomy types never have any luck at all, so spark up – the good vibes will bring you gambling success!

Officials' impact on results

In rugby league, and, to a lesser extent soccer, aussie rules and rugby union, the (mostly) men in the middle (ie. the referees and umpires), can have a bearing on results. Many a footy coach will claim that their precious team has a poor record under a particular referee or umpire. It can so mesmerise players on the day that it has just as much bearing on the result as injuries and weather conditions. It actually affects how a team approaches a game. It's that old psychological factor once again.

And the solution? This is totally out of your control, so don't even worry about it. Most of the perceived bias is imaginary in any case, and if there are allegations of bias it puts the officials in an uncomfortable position. Considering the difficulty of their job, it's an antagonism they probably do not deserve.

HOW, WHAT AND WHERE TO BET

In your slightly clammy grip, you have your weekly pay cheque. How much will you outlay on Manly, at 8 to 1 on, to beat Penrith at Brookvale? A bet with odds of 8 to 1 means a one dollar profit for your eight dollar investment, so one thousand dollars profit if you want to risk eight thousand. Mmmm. Maybe consider Geelong versus Richmond at Waverly? A far closer contest, offering better odds and a much better profit if you can stab the winner.

To make bets such as these you would venture to a bookmaker or to a legal betting operation such as the aforementioned Centrebet. Various TABs around the country generally offer a broader type of betting on the individual codes of football, some with the lure of great profit for a modest outlay.

For example, there is a system called 'Pick the Margins'. It's been in operation for several years and some of the dividends for a one dollar investment have been in excess of $250,000. It's simple, really. For example, if you wanted to pick the margins in rugby league, all you're required to do is pick whether side A is going to draw with, beat or be beaten by side B, and whether the margin will be between 1 and 12 points or more than 13.

The difficulty is, you have to make the correct decision on all matches in the round. It's wonderful listening to everybody in the office on Monday morning looking at their worthless 'pick the margins' card saying, 'I was going to pick Perth by 13 points, and if I'd just had Brisbane for a draw I'd be flying to Vegas this afternoon!' It's so, so easy with hindsight. Again, remember to do it for fun, then if you win it's great, but if you lose it's no great drama. The trauma sets in when you start to believe you don't need to work any more, and that your 'system' will pay dividends week in week out.

Other options

Week to week you can bet on games, scores and an entire round of matches. Who's going to win the Grand Final? Who's going to play in the Grand Final? Who's likely to win the Brownlow Medal? Who's going to win the Wooden Spoon? Who'll be the leading try scorer at Rugby's World Cup? Who'll kick the most goals in the AFL season, Ablett or Lockett? And when are they likely to boot their hundredth for the year? Who's going to win soccer's A League or the FA Cup?

All of these options require some incredible foresight and a large slab of luck. It's a bit like trying to find the winner of the Melbourne Cup in March. A lot can happen in the interim and throughout any season you should expect the unexpected – injuries, retirements, transfers, new coaches, etc.

If you're independently wealthy and can afford to have investments riding on a whim, then go right ahead. The old adage – 'bet what you can afford to lose' – isn't a bad rule to follow. If you have tendencies to get carried away by it all, then pick one type of bet each week and stick to that – whether it be the office tipping competition or whether you chose to pick the margins.

Luck

Are you lucky? Are biorhythms, the stars and the moon all on your side? Do you know when luck is in or out? Recognising these signs is one of life's mysteries every gambler is trying to unravel. Every system possible has been tested out by somebody at some time – for a while they'll work, then it's time to move on.

TIPPING COMPETITION STRATEGY

One of the great pleasures of the winter weeks is to fire in those tips and on Monday discover you've zoomed to the top of the office table. It gives you a wonderful warm feeling inside to know that you're beating die-hard footyheads at their own game. It can create havoc in the delicate balance of office politics, particularly if it's all the men you are beating, but who cares? You're in there to win, just like they are, regardless of whether a couple of egos get trampled in the process.

One of the most common mistakes made, though, when people hit the lead, is that they forget all about the strategy they used to get there and opt for all sorts of fancy tricks. This is the fastest way to fall off your perch. Sit tight and do exactly the same thing next week as you did last week and the week before. Never discard a winning technique.

Never panic if you're behind. Too often people charge from the back of the competition to the front and steal the prize you worked so hard for all year. Stick to your tried and tested formula. Don't go for the miracle results – that will, more than likely, send you tumbling to the embarrassing position of wooden spooner. In some offices they don't call it the wooden spoon, they call it the woman spoon cause it's most often females that are on the botom of the ladder. It's up to us to change that, isn't it?

Other little hints

Keep an eye on who's leading. This can assist your whole strategy. I'm not suggesting starting up an intimate affair so that they share their secrets with you, but just learn which teams they regularly support and you'll know which matches to gamble on in the hunt for valuable points. For example, they might have a very objective view on every game which has earnt them all the points, yet, because they support North Melbourne they pick North Melbourne every week even if it's obvious that Carlton at home, will be too tough for them. Heres your chance to earn a point that the competition leader might forfeit. The person winning is the only person you need be concerned about. Don't worry about anyone else anywhere on the ladder. They're inconsequential.

Don't let anybody pressure you. Tipping competitions are serious business for some, and they will try anything to throw you off a winning scent. The trick is to have your selections made before you get to the office. That way you can just hand in your teams and not have to debate your reasons for choosing them with somebody who's trying to tip you out of the running. Stay firm in your convictions!

Listen carefully to everything going on around you. A media interview with a coach or player can reveal a lot. Learn to recognise coaches' personality traits, then when they deviate from their normal attitudes you can guess that something is going on. If the coach is agitated, you can bet his team will be too. If the coach's mind isn't on the job, the players' minds won't be either. It will affect the game. Go for the opponents.

Ignore the hype surrounding teams. Often a good marketing executive or public relations director can evoke an aura around a team without the statistics to justify such a perception. If punters get caught up in this sort of hype they will go down! Stand back from the whizz-bang promotions and look at the facts. Is it a full strength team? Are the players all signed to the club for next season or are they dissatisfied and looking elsewhere? Use your intuition.

Whatever your formula, play on and have a ball!

(Note: if you start winning after these basic tips I'd appreciate a small piece of your earnings – say 10%?)

Who dares?

I guess there should be one word of warning before you head into a life of punting and tipping. The number of women seeking professional help for gambling problems over the last decade has risen dramatically, and is now surpassing the men. A degree of caution must go with your natural flamboyance.

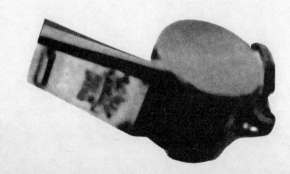

FULL TIME

THE FINAL WHISTLE

I t's time to blow the final whistle. I have the same sensation in my stomach now, as when I'm at the football and the countdown is on. I start getting all jumpy and nervous, hoping my team can sneak through a final goal to grab the lead; or at least hold the opposition back from scoring again so that the loss isn't too embarrassing. It's tough work being a footyhead sitting in the crowd! By now, you should know what I mean.

If nothing else, I hope you've learned to enjoy football. Like anything in life, it only takes a little bit of knowledge to whet your appetite and inspire you to learn more. The name of the game is fun. Without it, forget it.

There's a saying in sport, 'What happens on the field, stays on the field!' While I think it's designed to encourage players to leave any sporting hostilities on the ground, I think it has some relevance to us, as spectators.

The atmosphere and aura of sport is sensational. The energy absorbs you and you find yourself shouting as loudly as the person next to you, jumping as high as the kids in front, and stressing as badly as the teams on the field. It's inspiring. While the surroundings might inspire us to shout a few nasties at the referee, or make a couple of derogatory remarks about the opposition, they know and we know that it's heat of the moment stuff.

On the ground a couple of players might get caught up in a melee. One player might tackle another player a little too severely.

The referee might over react and award a penalty where perhaps a warning might have been sufficient. But once the hooter goes, the battle is over. Teams shake hands. Rivalries should be forgotten and celebration should take over.

It's the same for the crowd. We don't leave the football stadium carrying any particular grudge against either a player, a team, or a referee. As we leave the ground we reflect on the actions of all the people involved in the game; we might even have a few 'suggestions' for some of them. But that's where it stays.

We feel uplifted if our team has won, downhearted if it lost. We have been part of the team bonding. We shared every moment with the players and reacted to every decision made by the referee. We were there. Nothing can replace that feeling. The experience we take away from a game of football is one we can recall for years. Grand finals, internationals, World Cups, even the local derby between two traditional rivals will provide memories and moments that last a lifetime. Not only do we have those memories as personal ones, but we can share them with others who were also lucky enough to be a part of the scene.

I don't know of any other activity that brings people together like football and sport in general. People meet at a party or a work function and search for something in common as they try to strike up a conversation. How many times does it end up being footy? They were both at the AFL Grand Final street parade cheering on their heroes in the Carlton club. They were both at Australia's World Cup qualifier against Israel at the Sydney Football Stadium. They were both glued to their TV sets when South Africa made its triumphant return to the world of rugby. And they were both part of the supporters group that toured England on rugby league's last Kangaroo tour.

The memories are handed down through generations. Parents tell children, children tell their grandchildren, and the stories grow in stature every time they are told. A fairly ordinary game can end up being one of the most sensational ever played. A particular player who might have had the personality of a wet sock, but knew how to kick the ball home from 70 metres, ends up being one of the greats of the game.

Football lets all of us become champions. It lets all of us fantasise about how we would have played the game and how we would have scored the try. It gives us heroes who inspire us and motivate us. It gives us a release from day–to–day monotony which can sometimes sneak up on us.

I can't help thinking how empty life would be without football. As I sit here now, sharing some final thoughts with you, I look out of my window at the park across the road and I can see the kids playing football. I can hear their screams of triumph. I can see them acting the part of their chosen footballing hero. And I can see them growing up while they do it. Maybe one of them will become a champion footballer, maybe none of them will. But football has already taught them the joy of life.

Why don't you share the experience too?

GLOSSARY

aerial ping pong – *Nickname for aussie rules because of the frequent leaping into the air to take* **marks.**

around the corner – *Goal kicking technique based on soccer style using the instep rather than the toes.*

around the grounds – *Media term for on - air updates of scores from all games being played simultaneously around the country.*

away goal – *In qualifying games for major soccer competitions, such as the World Cup, if a visiting team scores a goal it is called an 'away goal' and it is worth two points rather than one.*

behind – *Minor score in aussie rules, made when the ball goes through the goalposts after being touched by a player or hitting one of the posts, or if a defending player puts it through, or if it rolls between one of the goal posts and one of the behind posts; behinds are worth a single point whereas goals are worth six points. Also means cute bottom.*

bench – *Area from where reserves, replacements and coaches watch the game.*

big game – *The ultimate, all important encounter. In reality, every game of football has become 'the big game'.*

blind side – *The side of play which is nearest to the* **touchline** *Also known as 'short side'.*

blood bin – *When a bleeding player temporarily leaves the field to have a wound attended to, the player is said to have gone to the blood bin.*

boundary umpire – *Aussie rules official who patrols the boundary line only.*

Brownlow Medal – *Aussie rulesí highest individual award for best and fairest player of the season.*

business–end – *Crunch time in a game or season.*

centre circle – *The heart of an aussie rules ground. A three metre circle inside the centre square where the umpires bounce the ball at the start, or re–start, of play.*

centre square – *Area in centre of aussie rules ground measuring 45 x 45 metres. Only four players from each side allowed in the area at the start, or re–start of play.*

charge – *Violent run straight at an opponent. In aussie rules, a frequent penalty.*

chip kick – *Quick, sharp kick – effective for getting the ball over the heads of defenders.*

conversion – *Successful kick at goal after a try has been scored in league and union. In soccer, penalties can be converted.*

corner kick – *Soccer kick taken from the corner of the field after the ball has been knocked over the goal line by a defender.*

dead ball line – *League and union boundary line running parallel to and behind the goal line, marking the* **in–goal area** *where tries are scored.*

differential penalty kick – *Penalty kick awarded for infringement in scrum. One cannot kick for goal from this penalty.*

direct free kick – *A kick straight at goal, awarded in soccer for an infringement by the opposition.*

double–header – *Two football games one after the other.*

dribble – *Soccer technique where a single player moves the ball down the field using a series of small, controlled kicks.*

drop kick – *A very precise kick in which a player drops the ball then kicks it a split second after it has been dropped to the ground. Also, an unfashionable person.*

drop punt – *A type of kick where the ball is dropped onto the player's boot and sent spinning end–over–end. A kick used for distance.*

dummy – *Feigning a pass to a teammate to bamboozle the opposition.*

dummy half – *A temporary position in league in which a player, known as the dummy half, stands behind a tackled player to receive the ball. See also* **play the ball.**

FA cup – *The Football Association Cup. English soccer's most prestigious trophy.*

feed the scrum – *The action of throwing the ball into the middle of a rugby league or union scrum.*

field goal – *A goal kicked during the run of play in league and union. Also known in union as drop–goal.*

field umpire – *Aussie rules official patrolling play in the field – as opposed to* **goal umpires** *and* **boundary umpires.**

FIFA – *Federation Internationale de Football Association. The world–wide controlling body of soccer.*

fixtures – *The week by week schedule of matches and venues.*

footyhead – *Person obsessed with football.*

form – *Term used to describe recent performances and overall condition of a player or team.*

free kick – *Kick awarded to one team after an infringement by the opposition.*

game plan – Pre–determined plan of attack and defence, orchestrated by the coach.

goal – A successful scoring kick.

goalie – Soccer goalkeeper.

goal line – The line on which goal posts stand.

goal square – Marking on an aussie rules field stretching nine metres out from the goal posts.

goal umpire – Aussie rules official who monitors the scoring of goals and behinds.

god – Gary Ablett

goose step – A stutter in runner's step to deceive a defending player. Made famous by David Campese.

grubber kick – Well placed kick where ball rolls along the ground.

handball – Aussie rules technique of punching a ball to a team mate.

handover – In league, after the team in possession has been tackled six times the ball must be handed over to the opposition. Also known as **turnover**.

hard yards – Term meaning 100% effort has been applied. Gaining ground on the field of play.

head high – A tackle made above a player's shoulders. Illegal in all codes because it can cause serious injury.

header – The soccer skill of directing the ball with the head.

held up – League or union term meaning that a try wasn't successful as the ball was not placed on the ground once over the goal line.

hill – Traditional non–grandstand area for crowd to gather. Renowned for containing the most vocal, and sometimes raucous, spectators.

home ground advantage – The atmosphere and conditions benefiting the club playing at their own ground.

indirect free kick – Penalty kick awarded in soccer. Apart from the kicker, the ball must be touched by at least one other teammate before a goal can be scored.

in–goal area – Rectangular area behind goal line where tries are scored in league and union.

jeer – Heckling, taunting, generally making rude remarks about a team, player or official during a game.

judiciary – Panel charged with adjudicating on serious, foul play.

kick for touch – Kicking the ball down the field to gain territorial advantage. The ball must bounce in bounds before crossing over the side or touch line.

king – Wally Lewis

knock–on – In league and union if the ball is accidentally fumbled forwards and hits the ground, a knock-on is called, resulting either in a scrum or in the handover of possession.

lazy Saturday – Day on which you are consumed by football – usually a **double–header** day.

line–out – Union formation where the forwards of both teams line up parallel to each other, and perpendicular to the **touchline** Forwards then jump for the ball which is thrown in by the hooker.

line–up – The roster of players selected for the next game.

linesman – A secondary official on the field of play patrolling the sidelines. Works with referee or umpire.

mark – To guard an opposition player. In aussie rules, a mark is a catch taken on the full from the kick of a player not less than 10 metres away. Marking adds much of the splendour to aussie rules football as players leap high to make the catch, appearing to walk on air.

marker – Player guarding an opponent.

maul – Rugby formation around the player with the ball as both sides battle for possession.

melee – Official word for brawling in aussie rules.

men in the middle – Term for the referees, umpires or other officials controlling a game.

mirrorball – Name for players more concerned with their looks than their game.

MLM – Men Looking for Melees. Applicable only to aussie rules. In other codes they are referred to as trouble–makers.

neville – Short for 'Neville Nobody'. Description of a no–name, or loser. Can be used as an expression of affection.

obstruction – When a player interferes with or upsets the general flow of play.

offside – Standing in an illegal position during play.

on a roll – Positive **form** resulting in a string of consecutive victories.

on the bench – On the team but as a substitute, or interchange player, as opposed to being named in the starting **line–up**.

open side – The side of play furthest from the **touchline**

own goal – Every soccer player's worst nightmare. When a player accidentally knocks the ball into his own team's net, scoring a point for the opposition.

pack – The forwards working as a team.

penalty – Advantage play awarded to one team for a foul incurred by the opposition.

penalty goal – Goal kicked following the awarding of a penalty.

place kick – *A kick when the ball is placed on the field (often on top of a little mound of sand specially carried on to the field in a bucket) and the player can kick without any interference. Used for* **conversion** *attempts or kick–off.*

play the ball – *In league when a tackled player rolls the ball off his foot and between his legs, to a waiting team mate who is called the* **dummy half.**

pretender – *A footy hoax.*

red card – *Shown to a soccer player for a severe offence, resulting in an immediate send–off.*

referee – *Controlling official on the field of play in league, union and soccer.*

report – *Aussie rules umpires may write down the number of a player who has committed a punishable offence such as striking, charging, abusive language or racial abuse.*

ruck – *Rugby union formation around player tackled to the ground who must release the ball immediately.*

ruggers – *A slang term for union players.*

runner – *Aussie rules coach's messenger who runs information to the players during a game.*

sacred turf – *Hallowed playing ground made legendary by the heroes and forefathers of football.*

salary cap – *Amount set by the sport's governing body for the total amount each club is allowed to spend on players' salaries.*

scrum – *Where the forward packs of both teams come together to contest for possession of the ball.*

send–off – *The expulsion of a player from the game.*

shepherding – *Interfering by following or guarding an opponent too closely. Legal in aussie rules only, if player is not more than 5 metres away from the ball.*

shot at goal – *Kick for goal.*

sideline expert – *A spectator who knows, or thinks she does, more than the experts playing the game.*

sideline eye – *A media commentator who patrols the boundary line during match coverage.*

side–step – *A sharp movement to the left or right to elude an opponent.*

sin bin – *A term for a ten minute send–off for a misdemeanour.*

slide tackle – *A tackle used in soccer where a defending player effectively slides towards an opponent with the ball.*

SNAF – *Sensitive new age footyhead.*

spoiler – *An aussie rules player who knocks the ball away from an opponent attempting to take a mark.*

substitute – *A player taking the place of another on the field who goes off tired or injured or whom the coach decides should take a break.*

sudden death – *A method of determining the winner of a game when normal time is over and the score is drawn. An extra period of play in which the first team to score, wins.*

State of Origin – *Annual series between state representative teams rather than clubs.*

stats – *Short for match statistics.*

swerve ball – *A kicked ball that travels in an arc – used for getting around a line of defence in soccer.*

system – *A strategy used for tipping or gambling.*

tackle – *A challenge made on an opponent with the ball.*

test – *An international match – nation versus nation.*

throw in – *A way of getting the ball back in play after it has gone over the* **touchline** *or the boundary line.*

time on– *A period of time added to the end of each quarter in aussie rules to make up for stoppages during play because of injuries, penalties or melees.*

torpedo kick – *A kick used for great distances – the ball is kicked at an angle to send it spiralling forwards.*

touch footy – *Non–contact football game based on elements of league and union.*

touch in goal – *The part of the* **touchline** *between the goal line and the dead ball line.*

touch judge – *League and union officials who patrol the* **touchline** *or side– lines.*

touchline – *The sideline boundary of a playing field.*

tribunal – *A panel established to adjudicate on serious foul play.*

try – *Placing the ball over the opposition's goal line. Tries are the major way of earning points in league and union.*

turnover – *See* **handover.**

umpire – *The aussie rules official on the field of play. Only aussie rules uses the term umpire; the other codes have referees.*

volley – *Kicking a ball on the full.*

wally – *Goose, fool, wanker.*

wooden spoon – *Prize for finishing last in a competition.*

yellow card – *Cautionary card shown to soccer player for infringing on the rules. Two yellow cards result in a* **send–off.**

Bellew, Tom, *An Introduction To Rugby League*, The International Rules Committee.

Brasch, R., *How Did Sports Begin*, Fontana/Collins, Sydney, 1986.

Corcoran, Peter, *The Name Of The Game Is Rugby League*, Aussie Sports Books, Sydney, 1991.

Dunstan, Keith, *Sports*, Sun Books, Melbourne, 1981.

Federation Internationali de Football, *FIFA Laws Of The Game*, Federation Internationali de Football Association, Switzerland, 1994.

Fleming, Jim, and Brian Anderson, *The New Rugby Union Laws Explained*, ABC Enterprises, Sydney, 1992.

Heads, Ian, *True Blue – The Story Of The NSW Rugby League*, Ironbark Press, Sydney, 1992.

Hobbs, Greg, *Australian Football – A Fundamental Guide To The Game*, Progress Press.

James, Chris, *The Name Of The Game Is Soccer*, Aussie Sport Books, Sydney, 1991.

McGowan, Bill, Patricia McDonald and Philip Derriman – Editors, *The ABC Grandstand Guide to 101 Sports*, ABC Enterprises, Sydney, 1992.

O'Neil, David, *Pick Me Up And Run, A Simple Guide To Rugby*, Winky Press, Sydney, 1994.

Pascoe, Robert, *The Winter Game – The Complete History*, The Text Publishing Company, Melbourne, 1995.

Rugby Football League, *Rugby League – Know The Game*, A & C Black, London, 1994.

Warren, John, *Australian Rules Football*, Cambridge University Press, Melbourne, 1988.